# BARMANS' A-Z GUIDE TO
# COCKTAILS

C000004210

NEW
HOLLAND

Published by New Holland Publishers
London • Sydney • Cape Town • Auckland
www.newhollandpublishers.com

Garfield House 86–88 Edgware Road London W2 2EA United Kingdom
1/66 Gibbes Street Chatswood NSW 2067 Australia
Wembley Square First Floor Solan Road Gardens Cape Town 8001 South Africa
218 Lake Road Northcote Auckland New Zealand

A catalogue record of this book is available at the British Library and the
National Library of Australia.

ISBN 9781742573380

Printed by: Toppan Leefung Printing Limited

# Table of Contents

# Introduction

## METHODS OF MIXING COCKTAILS

The four methods below are the most common processes of mixing cocktails:-

**1.** Shake      **2.** Stir

**3.** Build      **4.** Blend

**1. SHAKE:** To shake is to mix a cocktail by shaking it in a cocktail shaker by hand. First, fill the glass part of the shaker three quarters full with ice, then pour the ingredients on top of the ice. Less expensive ingredients are usually poured before the deluxe ingredients. Pour the contents of the glass into the metal part of the shaker and shake vigorously for ten to fifteen seconds. Remove the glass section and using a Hawthorn strainer, strain contents into the cocktail glass. Shaking ingredients that do not mix easily with spirits is easy and practical ( eg juices, egg whites, cream and sugar syrups).

Most shakers have two or three parts. In a busy bar, the cap is often temporarily misplaced. If this happens, a coaster or the inside palm of your hand is quite effective. American shakers are best.

To sample the cocktail before serving to the customer, pour a small amount into the shaker cap and using a straw check the taste.

**2. STIR:** To stir a cocktail is to mix the ingredients by stirring them with ice in a mixing glass and then straining them into a chilled cocktail glass. Short circular twirls are most preferred. (NB. The glass part of a shaker will do well for this.) Spirits, liqueurs and vermouths that blend easily together are mixed by this method.

**3. BUILD:** To build a cocktail is to mix the ingredients in the glass in which the cocktail is to be served, floating one on top of the other. Hi-ball, long fruit juice and carbonated mixed cocktails are typically built using this technique. Where possible a swizzle stick should be put into the drink to mix the ingredients after being presented to the customer. Long straws are excellent substitutes when swizzle sticks are unavailable.

**4. BLEND:** To blend a cocktail is to mix the ingredients using an electric blender/mixer. It is recommended to add the fruit (fresh or tinned) first. Slicing small pieces gives a smoother texture than if you add the whole fruit. Next, pour the alcohol. Ice should always be added last. This order ensures that the fruit is blended freely with the alcoholic ingredients and allows the ice to gradually mix into the beverage, chilling the flavour. Ideally, the blender should be on for at least 20 seconds. Following this procedure will prevent ice and fruit lumps that then need to be strained.

If the blender starts to rattle and hum, ice may be obstructing the blades from spinning. Always check that the blender is clean before you start. Angostura Bitters is ammonia based which is suitable for cleaning. Fill 4 to 5 shakes with hot water, rinse and then wipe clean.

## TECHNIQUES IN MAKING COCKTAILS

**1. SHAKE AND POUR:** After shaking the cocktail, pour the contents straight into the glass. When pouring into hi-ball glasses and some old-fashioned glasses the ice cubes are included. This eliminates straining.

**2. SHAKE AND STRAIN:** Using a Hawthorn strainer (or knife) this technique prevents the ice going into the glass. Straining protects the cocktail ensuring melted ice won't dilute the flavour and mixture.

**3. FLOAT INGREDIENTS:** Hold the spoon right way up and rest it with the lip slightly above the level of the last layer. Fill spoon gently and the contents will flow smoothly from all around the rim. Use the back of the spoon's dish only if you are experienced.

**4. FROSTING (sugar and salt rims):** This technique is used to coat the rim of the glass with either salt or sugar. First, rub lemon/orange slice juice all the way around the glass rim. Next, holding the glass upside down by the stem, rest on a plate containing salt or sugar and turn slightly so that it adheres to the glass. Pressing the glass too deeply into the salt or sugar often results in chunks sticking to the glass. A lemon slice is used for salt and an orange slice is used for sugar.

To achieve colour affects, put a small amount of grenadine or coloured liqueur in a plate and coat the rim of the glass, then gently place in the sugar. The sugar absorbs the grenadine, which turns it pink. This is much easier than mixing grenadine with sugar and then trying to get it to stick to the glass.

## HELPFUL HINTS

Cocktail mixing is an art which is expressed in the preparation and presentation of the cocktail.

## HOW TO MAKE A BRANDY ALEXANDER CROSS

Take two short straws and, with a sharp knife, slice one of the straws half way through in the middle and wedge the other uncut straw into the cut straw to create a cross.

## STORING FRUIT JUICES

Take a 750mL bottle and soak it in hot water to remove the label and sterilise the alcohol. The glass has excellent appeal and you'll find it easier to pour the correct measurement with an attached nip pourer.

## SUGAR SYRUP RECIPE

Fill a cup or bowl (depending on how much you want to make) with white sugar, top it up with boiling water until the receptacle is just about full and keep stirring until the sugar is fully dissolved. Refrigerate when not in use. Putting a teaspoon of sugar into a cocktail is being lazy, it does not do the job properly as the sugar just dissolves.

## JUICE TIPS

Never leave juices, coconut cream or other ingredients in cans. Pour them into clean bottles, cap and refrigerate them. All recipes in this book have been tested with Berri fruit juices.

## ICE

Ice is probably the most important part of cocktails. It is used in nearly all cocktails. Consequently ice must be clean and fresh at all times.

The small square cubes and flat chips of ice are superior for chilling and mixing cocktails. Ice cubes with holes are inefficient. Wet ice, ice scraps and broken ice should only be used in blenders.

## CRUSHED ICE

Take the required amount of ice and fold into a clean linen cloth. Although uncivilised, the most effective method is to smash it against the bar floor. Shattering with a bottle may break the bottle. Some retailers sell portable ice crushers. Alternatively a blender may be used. Half fill with ice and then pour water into the blender until it reaches the level of the ice. Blend for about 30 seconds, strain out the water and you have perfectly crushed ice. Always try and use a metal scoop to collect the ice from the ice tray.

Never pick up the ice with your hands. This is unhygienic. Shovelling the glass into the ice tray to gather ice can also cause breakages and hence should be avoided where possible.

It is important that the ice tray is cleaned each day. As ice is colourless and odourless, many people assume wrongly it is always clean. Taking a cloth soaked in hot water, wipe the inside of the bucket warm. The blenders used for all of our bar requirements are Moulinex blenders with glass bowls. We have found these blenders to be of exceptional quality.

## GLASSES

| | | | |
|---|---|---|---|
| Bacchus Wine Glass: | 200mL | | |
| Brandy balloon: | 650mL 650mL | Hurricane: | 200mL, 250mL, 400mL, |
| Champagne flute: | 140mL, 180mL | Irish coffee: | 250mL |
| Champagne saucer: | 140mL, 250mL | Margarita: | 260mL |
| Cocktail glass: | 90mL, 125mL, 140mL | Martini glass: | 90mL |
| Cordial (Embassy): | 30mL | Old-fashioned spirit: | 185mL, 200mL, 290mL |
| Cordial (Lexington): | 37mL | Poco/viva grande: | 380mL |
| Fancy cocktail: | 250mL, 285mL | Salud grande: | 290mL |
| Fancy Hi-Ball: | 220mL, 360mL, 500mL | Tall Dutch cordial: | 45mL |
| Fiesta grande: | 350mL, 490mL | Tulip champagne: | 145mL, 170mL |
| Footed Hi-Ball: | 285mL, 300mL | Whisky shot: | 45mL, 60mL |
| Hi-Ball: | 250mL, 270mL, 285mL, 360mL | Wine goblet: | 140mL, 190mL |

A proven method to cleaning glasses is to hold each glass individually over a bucket of boiling water until the glass becomes steamy and then with a clean linen cloth rub in a circular way to ensure the glass is polished for the next serve.

Cocktails can be poured into any glass but the better the glass the better the appearance of the cocktail.

One basic rule should apply and that is, use no coloured glasses as they spoil the appearance of cocktails. All glasses have been designed for a specific task, eg.,

1. Hi-Ball glasses for long cool refreshing drinks.

2. Cocktail glasses for short, sharp, or stronger drinks.

3. Champagne saucers for creamy after-dinner style drinks, etc.

The stem of the glass has been designed so you may hold it whilst polishing, leaving the bowl free of marks and germs so that you may enjoy your drink. All cocktail glasses should be kept in a refrigerator or filled with ice while you are preparing the cocktails in order to chill the glass. An appealing affect on a 90ml cocktail glass can be achieved by running the glass under cold water and then placing it in the freezer.

# Introduction

## GARNISHES AND JUICES

Almonds
Apple juice
Apricot conserve
Banana
Blueberries
Carbonated waters
Celery
Celery salt
Chocolate flake
Cinnamon
Coconut cream
Cream
Crushed Pineapple
Cucumber
Eggs
Flowers (assorted)
Jelly Babies
Lemon juice
Lemons
Lime juice
Limes
Milk
Mint leaves
Nutmeg
Olives
Onions
Orange and mango juice
Orange juice
Oranges
Pepper
Pineapple
Pineapple juice
Red cocktail onions
Red maraschino cherries
Rockmelon
Salt
Strawberries
Sugar
Sugar cubes
Sugar syrup
Tabasco sauce
Tinned fruit
Tinned nectars
Tinned pulps
Tomato
Vanilla ice cream
Worcestershire sauce

Simplicity is the most important fact to keep in mind when garnishing cocktails. Do not overdo the garnish; make it striking, but if you can't get near the cocktail to drink it then you have failed. Most world champion cocktails just have a lemon slice, or a single red cherry.

Tall refreshing Hi-Balls tend to have more garnish as the glass is larger. A swizzle stick should nearly always be served in long cocktails. Straws are always served for a lady, but optional for a man.

Plastic animals, umbrellas, fans and a whole variety of novelty goods are now available to garnish with, and they add a lot of fun to the drink.

## ALCOHOL RECOMMENDED FOR A COCKTAIL BAR
### Spirits

Bourbon
Brandy
Campari
Canadian club
Gin
Malibu
Ouzo
Pernod
Rum
Scotch
Southern comfort
Tennessee whisky
Tequila
Vandermint
Vodka

# Introduction

## Liqueurs

Advocaat
Amaretto
Bailey's Irish cream
Banana
Benedictine
Blue curaçao
Cassis
Chartreuse – green and yellow
Cherry advocaat
Cherry brandy
Clayton's tonic (Non-alcoholic)
Coconut
Cointreau
Crème de café
Crème de menthe – green
Dark crème de cacao

Drambuie
Frangelico
Galliano
Grand Marnier
Kahlúa
Kirsch
Mango
Melon
Orange
Peach
Pimm's
Sambuca – clear
Sambuca – black
Strawberry
Triple Sec

## Vermouth

Cinzano Bianco
Cinzano Dry
Cinzano Rosso

Martini Bianco
Martini Dry
Martini Rosso

## ESSENTIAL EQUIPMENT FOR A COCKTAIL BAR

Bottle openers
Can-opener
Coasters and serviettes
Cocktail shaker
Free pourers
Hand cloths for cleaning glasses
Hawthorn strainer
Ice bucket
Ice scoop

Knife, cutting board
Measures (jiggers)
Mixing glass
Moulinex electric blender
Scooper spoon (long teaspoon)
Spoon with muddler
Swizzle sticks, straws
Waiter's friend corkscrew

## DESCRIPTION OF LIQUEURS AND SPIRITS

**Advocaat:** A combination of fresh egg whites, yolks, sugar, brandy, vanilla and spirit. Limited shelf life. Recommended shelf life 12–15 months from date of manufacture.

**Amaretto:** A rich subtle liqueur with a unique almond flavour.

**Angostura Bitters:** An essential part of any bar or kitchen. A unique additive whose origins date back to 1824. A mysterious blend of natural herbs and spices, both a seasoning and flavouring agent, in both sweet and savoury dishes and drinks. Ideal for dieters as it is low in sodium and calories.

# Introduction

**Aquavit:** Made in Scandinavia, it is distilled from a grain or potato mash and flavoured with such flavourings as caraway, cumin and cardamom.

**Bailey's Irish Cream:** The largest selling liqueur in the world. It is a blend of Irish whisky, softened by Irish cream and other flavourings. It is a natural product.

**Banana:** Fresh ripe bananas are the perfect base for the definitive daiquiri and a host of other exciting fruit cocktails.

**Benedictine:** A perfect end to a perfect meal. Serve straight, with ice, soda, or as part of a favourite cocktail.

**Bourbon:** Has a smooth, deep, easy flavour.

**Brandy:** Smooth and mild spirit, is considered very smooth and palatable, ideal for mixing.

**Campari:** A drink for many occasions, both as a long or short drink, or as a key ingredient in many fashionable cocktails.

**Cassis:** Deep, rich purple promises and delivers a regal and robust flavour and aroma. Cassis lends itself to neat drinking or an endless array of delicious sauces and desserts.

**Chartreuse:** A liqueur available in either yellow or green colour. Made by the monks of the Carthusian order. The only world famous liqueur still made by monks.

**Cherry Advocaat:** Same as Advocaat, plus natural cherry flavours and colour is added.

**Cherry Brandy:** Is made from concentrated, morello cherry juice. Small quantity of bitter almonds and vanilla is added to make it more enjoyable as a neat drink before or after dinner. Excellent for mixers, topping, ice cream, fruit salads, pancakes, etc.

**Coconut:** A smooth liqueur, composed of exotic coconut, heightened with light-bodied white rum.

**Cointreau:** Made from a neutral grain spirit, as opposed to cognac. An aromatic flavour of natural citrus fruits. A great mixer or delightful over ice.

**Crème de cacao – dark:** Rich, deep chocolate. Smooth and classy. Serve on its own, or mix for all kinds of delectable treats.

**Crème de cacao – white:** This liqueur delivers a powerfully lively, full bodied chocolate flavour. Excellent ingredient when absence of colour is desired.

**Crème de Grand Marnier:** A blend of Grand Marnier and smooth French cream. A premium product, a very smooth taste with the orange/cognac flavour blending beautifully with smooth cream. Introduced to Australia in 1985.

**Crème de menthe – green:** Clear peppermint flavour, reminiscent of a fresh, crisp, clean winter's day in the mountains. Excellent mixer, a necessity in the gourmet kitchen.

# Introduction

**Crème de menthe – white:** As Crème de menthe – green, when colour is not desired.

**Curaçao – blue:** Same as Triple Sec, brilliant blue colour is added to make some cocktails more exciting.

**Curaçao – orange:** Again, same as above, but stronger in orange, colouring is used for other varieties of cocktail mixers.

**Curaçao Triple Sec:** Based on natural citrus fruits. Well known fact is citrus fruits are the most important aromatic flavour constituents. Interesting to know citrus fruit was known 2000 years before Christ. As a liqueur one of the most versatile. Can be enjoyed with or without ice as a neat drink, or used in mixed cocktails more than any other liqueur. Triple Sec – also known as white curaçao.

**Galliano:** The distinguished taste! A classic liqueur that blends with a vast array of mixed drinks.

**Gin:** Its aroma comes from using the highest quality juniper berries and other rare and subtle herbs. Perfect mixer for both short and long drinks.

**Kirsch:** A fruit brandy distilled from morello cherries. Delicious drunk straight and excellent in a variety of food recipes.

**Drambuie:** A Scotch whisky liqueur. Made from a secret recipe dating back to 1745. "Dram Buidheach" the drink that satisfies.

**Frangelico:** A precious liqueur imported from Italy. Made from wild hazelnuts with infusions of berries and flowers to enrich the flavour.

**Grand Marnier:** An original blend of fine old cognac and an extract of oranges. The recipe is over 150 years old

**Kahlúa:** A smooth, dark liqueur made from real coffee and fine clear spirits. Its origins are based in Mexico.

**Malibu:** A clear liqueur based on white rum with the subtle addition of coconut. Its distinctive taste blends naturally with virtually every mixer available.

**Melon Liqueur:** Soft green, exudes freshness. Refreshing and mouthwatering honeydew melon. Simple yet complex. Smooth on the palate, serve on the rocks, or use to create summertime cocktails.

**Ouzo:** The traditional spirit aperitif of Greece. The distinctive flavour is derived mainly from the seed of the anise plant. A neutral grain spirit distilled in Australia.

**Peach:** The flavour of fresh peaches and natural peach juice make this a cocktail lover's dream.

**Peachtree Schnapps:** Crystal clear, light liqueur, bursting with the taste of ripe peaches. Drink chilled, on the rocks or mix with any soft drink or juice.

**Pineapple:** A just ripe, sun-filled delight. Delicious neat, a necessity for summertime cocktails.

# Introduction

**Rum:** A smooth, dry, light bodied rum, especially suited for drinks in which you require subtle aroma and delicate flavour.

**Rye Whiskey:** Distilled from corn, rye and malted barley. A light, mild and delicate whiskey, ideal for drinking straight or in mixed cocktails.

**Sabra:** A unique jaffa flavour which comes from tangy oranges, with a hint of chocolate.

**Sambuca – clear:** The Italian electric taste experience. Made from elder berries with a touch of anise.

**Sambuca – black:** An exciting encounter between Sambuca di Galliano and extracts of black elderberry.

**Scotch Whisky –** A blended whisky.

**Southern Comfort:** A liqueur not a bourbon as often thought. It is a unique, full-bodied liqueur with a touch of sweetness. Its recipe is a secret, but it is known to be based on peaches and apricots. It is the largest selling liqueur in Australia.

**Strawberry:** Fluorescent red, unmistakable strawberry bouquet. Natural liqueur delivers a true to nature, fresh strawberry flavour.

**Tennessee Whisky :** Contrary to popular belief, this is not a bourbon, it is a distinctive product called Tennessee Whisky. Made from the 'old sour mash' process. Leached through hard maple charcoal, then aged in charred white oak barrels, at a controlled temperature, acquiring body, bouquet and colour, yet remaining smooth.

**Tequila:** Distilled from the Mexcal variety of the cacti plant. A perfect mixer or drink straight with salt and lemon.

**Tia Maria:** A liqueur with a cane spirit base, and its flavour derived from the finest Jamaican coffee. It is not too sweet with a subtle taste of coffee.

**Vandermint:** A rich chocolate liqueur with the added zest of mint.

**Vermouth:** By description, vermouth is a herbally infused wine.

Three styles are most prevalent, these are:

> **Rosso:** A bitter sweet herbal flavour, often drunk as an aperitif.

> **Bianco:** Is light, fruity and refreshing. Mixes well with soda, lemonade and fruit juices.

> **Dry:** Is crisp, light and dry and is used as a base for many cocktails.

**Vodka:** The second largest selling spirit in the world. Most vodkas are steeped in tanks containing charcoal, removing all odours and impurities, making a superior quality product.

**Triple Sec:** See Blue Curaçao.

# Aberdeen Angus

## Ingredients

**Glass:**   140mL cocktail glass
**Mixers:**   30mL Scotch whisky
             10mL Drambuie
             1 tablespoon honey
             10mL fresh lime juice

## Method

Mix honey into Scotch whisky and add lime then warm drambuie over a low flame and pour.

**Garnish:** Plastic bull.

# Acapulco

## Ingredients

**Glass:**  150mL old-fashioned spirit glass
**Mixers:** 30mL Bacardi
10mL Cointreau
1 egg white
15mL fresh lime juice
add sugar to taste

## Method

Shake over ice and pour.

**Garnish:** Partially torn mint leaves.

# Alabama Slammer

## Ingredients

**Glass:** whisky shot

**Mixers:** 10mL gin
10mL Amaretto
10mL orange juice
10mL southern comfort

## Method

Pour in order then shoot. A real drink! From the heart of the Deep South, USA.

# Alaska

**Ingredients**

**Glass:** 90mL cocktail glass

**Mixers:** 30mL gin
10mL yellow Chartreuse
1–2 dashes of orange curaçao

**Method**

Shake over ice and strain.

**Garnish:** Orange twist.

# Almond Orange Frost

### Ingredients

**Glass:** 250mL Champagne saucer

**Mixers:** 15mL Amaretto
15mL Frangelico
15mL Chambord
10mL fresh lime juice
10mL fresh lemon juice
2 scoops orange sorbet

### Method

Blend with ice.

**Garnish:** Orange slice.

# Americano

## Ingredients

**Glass:** 285mL hi-ball glass

**Mixers:** 30mL Campari
30mL rosso vermouth
top up with soda water

## Method

Build over ice and top up with soda water.

**Garnish:** Orange slice.

**Comments:** Originated from European travellers visiting America desiring a taste of European aperitifs.

# Aqua Thunder

## Ingredients

**Glass:** 285mL hi-ball glass

**Mixers:** 10mL blue curaçao
10mL banana liqueur
30mL melon liqueur
10mL freshly squeezed lemon
top up with soda water

## Method

Build over ice.

**Garnish:** Swizzle stick, and slice of lemon.

**Comments:** Watch in wonder as the soda water waterfall splashes over the ice creating a thunderous aqua-coloured spectacular.

# Aquavit Fiz

## Ingredients

**Glass:**   170mL tulip champagne glass

**Mixers:**  45mL Aquavit
30mL lemon juice
15mL cherry schnapps
10mL sugar syrup
1 egg white
top up with soda water

## Method

Shake over ice and strain then top up with soda water.

**Garnish:** A red cherry.

# Absolut Cosmopolitan

### Ingredients

**Glass:**  90mL martini glass (chilled)

**Mixers:**  45mL Absolut Citron
20mL triple sec
20mL cranberry juice
juice of ½ fresh Lime

### Method

Shake with ice and strain into chilled martini glass.

**Garnish:** Orange twist.

**Comments:** A citrus tasting masterpiece. A very pleasant cocktail, destined to be a classic.

# Absolut Iceberg

## Ingredients

**Glass:** 285mL hi-ball glass

**Mixers:** 30mL Absolut Citron
15mL triple sec
150mL bitter lemon

## Method

Pour Absolut Citron and triple sec over ice into a chilled highball glass and top with Bitter Lemon.

**Garnish:** Orange slice.

**Comments:** A delightful long citrus drink for a hot day.

# Australian Gold

## Ingredients

**Glass:** 90mL cocktail glass

**Mixers:** 30mL rum
30mL mango liqueur
30mL Galliano

## Method

Build over ice.

**Garnish:** 1 small pineapple wedge.

**Comments:** This straight spirit cocktail is also known as "Queensland Wine".

# B & B

## Ingredients

**Glass:**   brandy balloon

**Mixers:**  30mL Martell cognac
30mL Benedictine

## Method

Build, no ice.

**Garnish:** None.

**Comments:** Tempt your pallet with this historical blend of choice liqueurs. Relaxing by the fire on winter nights, the genuine connoisseur will enjoy this drink over interesting conversation with friends. Ideal with coffee.

# Banana Colada

## Ingredients

**Glass:** 285mL fancy cocktail glass

**Mixers:** 30mL Bacardi
30mL sugar syrup
30mL coconut cream
30mL cream
120mL pineapple juice
half a sliced banana

## Method

Build with ice and pour.

**Garnish:** Slice of banana, pineapple spear and mint leaves. Serves with straws.

**Comments:** A simple exemplary cocktail to demonstrate the variety of fruits available, particularly in Australia. Be adventurous and surprise yourself!

# Banana Daiquiri

### Ingredients

**Glass:**  140mL champagne saucer

**Mixers:**  three quarters of a sliced banana
30mL sugar syrup
30mL Bacardi
30mL lemon juice

### Method

Blend with ice and strain.

**Garnish :** Round slice of banana and mint leaves.

**Comments :** Frequently served on arrival at cocktail parties, this icy cold mixture is always warmly received by guests. Simple to prepare in large quantities, different combinations of fruits can be added to the base mix without deliberation. Adjust measurements of lemon and sugar accordingly for a sweeter or sour taste. Where unripe fruit is used, fruit liqueurs will help enrich the flavour.

# Bananarama

## Ingredients

**Glass:** 140mL cocktail glass

**Mixers:** 30mL vodka
30mL Kahlúa
15mL Bailey's Irish Cream
1 banana
60mL cream

## Method

Blend with ice and pour.

**Garnish:** Two banana slices wedged on rim of glass.

**Comments:** A delightful cocktail, drunk on North Queensland island resorts, where tourists dance the "RAMA".

# Bermuda Rose

### Ingredients

**Glass:** 90mL cocktail glass

**Mixers:** 30mL gin
10mL lime juice
1 teaspoon grenadine
4–5 drops of apricot brandy

### Method

Shake over ice and strain.

**Garnish:** A slice of lime.

# Between The Sheets

## Ingredients

**Glass:**    140mL champagne saucer

**Mixers:**  30mL brandy
30mL Bacardi
30mL Cointreau
15mL lemon juice

## Method

Shake with ice and strain.

**Garnish:** Lemon slice and twist.

**Comments:** A pre-dinner cocktail. A fine blend of traditional spirits for the mature palate.

# Black Opal

## Ingredients

**Glass:**  90mL cocktail glass

**Mixers:**  15mL black Sambuca
15mL Cointreau
15mL Bailey's Irish Cream
15mL cream

## Method

Build black Sambuca and Cointreau then light. Next, pour Baileys and cream over flaming ingredients.

**Garnish:** None.

**Comments:** A novel demonstration of lifestyle cocktails – the heat of the flame illuminates the black Sambuca.

# Black Russian

## Ingredients

**Glass:**   200mL old-fashioned spirit glass

**Mixers:** 30mL vodka
            30mL Kahlúa

## Method

Build over ice.

**Garnish:** Swizzle stick.

**Comments:** Superb after dinner as vodka lubricates the way for the scrumptious chocolate Kahlúa. Add a dollop of cream on top of cola in a hi-ball glass to stretch the drink.

Tia Maria or dark crème de cacao may be substituted for Kahlúa, making the drink a **"Black Pearl"**.

# Bloody Mary

## Ingredients

**Glass:** 285ml hi-ball glass

**Mixers:** 30mL vodka
Worcestershire sauce to taste
120mL tomato juice
Tabasco sauce to taste

salt and pepper to taste
celery salt, optional

## Method

Build or shake over ice and strain.

**Garnish:** Stick of celery, slice of lemon.

**Comments:** Remember to add the spices first, then vodka followed by tomato juice. Lemon juice and slices are optional ingredients. The celery stick is not just part of the garnish, so feel free to nibble as you drink. The glass may also be salt-rimmed. A **"Virgin Mary"** is non alcoholic, with no vodka added. A **"Bloody Maria"** replaces vodka with tequila. Also referred to as a **"Stomach Settler"** or **"Livener"**.

# Blue Bayou

## Ingredients

**Glass:**   285mL hi-ball glass

**Mixers:**   15mL Galliano
15mL dry vermouth
30mL gin
15m blue curaçao
top up with lemonade

## Method

Shake with ice and pour.

**Garnish:** Lemon slice and mint leaves. Swizzle stick and straws.

**Comments:** A prize-winning cocktail, which is very refreshing. Perfect for outdoor parties. The yellow of the Galliano can tend to turn the blue curaçao slightly aqua-green in colour.

# Blueberry Delight

## Ingredients

**Glass:** 140mL cocktail glass

**Mixers:** 30mL black Sambuca
20mL coconut liqueur
10m strawberry liqueur
60mL cream

## Method

Shake with ice and strain.

**Garnish:** Strawberry on side of glass with blueberries on a toothpick.

**Comments:** Find your thrills on these strawberry and blueberry hills.

# Blue French

## Ingredients

**Glass:** 285mL hi-ball glass

**Mixers:** 30mL pernod
10mL blue curaçao
1 teaspoon lemon juice
top up with bitter lemon

## Method

Build over ice and stir.

**Garnish:** Lemon slice on side of glass, swizzle stick and straws.

**Comments:** A great thirst quencher. Ideal when relaxing by the pool.

# Blue Hawaii

## Ingredients

**Glass:** 285mL hi-ball glass
**Mixers:** 30mL Bacardi
30mL blue curaçao
60mL pineapple juice
30mL lemon juice
30mL sugar syrup

## Method

Build over ice and pour.

**Garnish:** Pineapple wedge, and half strawberry.
Serve with a straw.

**Comments:** A favourite Hawaiian drink. The mixing of pineapple juice and blue curaçao tends to turn the cocktail aqua-green in colour.

# Bolshoi Punch

### Ingredients

**Glass:** 285ml footed hi-ball glass

**Mixers:** 30mL vodka
10mL dark rum
10mL crème de cassis
15mL lime juice
15mL lemon juice
top up with bitter lemon

### Method

Blend with ice and strain then top up with bitter lemon.

**Garnish:** An orange slice and red cherry.

# Bombay Punch

## Ingredients
**Glass:** 285mL footed hi-ball glass
**Mixers:** 30mL cognac
10mL dry sherry
10mL Cointreau
10mL maraschino
20mL lemon juice
top up with soda water or champagne

## Method
Blend with ice and strain then top up with soda or champagne.

**Garnish:** A red cherry and orange slice.

# Bosom Caresser

## Ingredients
**Glass:** 140mL champagne saucer
**Mixers:** 30mL brandy
15mL orange liqueur
1 teaspoon grenadine
1 egg yolk

## Method
Shake with ice and strain.

**Garnish:** Two red cherries, slit on side of glass.

**Comments:** Close to every lady's heart! Egg yolk allows the cocktail to breathe supporting the brandy's body and bounce. Fine on any occasion.

# Boston Cream

### Ingredients

**Glass:** 125mL cocktail glass, frosted

**Mixers:** 30mL cream
15mL triple sec
30mL coconut cream
15mL grenadine

### Method

Shake over ice and strain.

**Garnish:** A chocolate cross.

# Brandy Alexander

## Ingredients

**Glass:** 140mL champagne saucer

**Mixers:** 30mL brandy
30mL dark crème de cacao
1 teaspoon grenadine
30mL cream

## Method

Shake with ice and strain.

**Garnish:** Sprinkle of nutmeg and a cherry.

**Comments:** An after-dinner cocktail. See 'Helpful Hints' for an easy step-by-step guide on how to make a Brandy Alexander cross'. An **"Alexander"** replaces the cacao with green crème de menthe. Cognac may be substituted for brandy to deliver an exceptional aftertaste.

# Cafe Nero

## Ingredients
**Glass:** 140mL champagne saucer
**Mixers:** 30mL Galliano
black coffee
fresh cream
sugar

## Method
Build, no ice. Firstly, sprinkle white sugar inside the glass after coating with Galliano. Set Galliano alight and twirl the glass so that flames burn brightly. Pour black coffee gently into glass then layer cream on top of the burning coffee. Sprinkle grated chocolate over the coffee.

**Garnish:** Grated chocolate.

**Comments:** Named after Emperor Nero of Rome. Also called a **"Roman Coffee"**. Coffee may be served on an accompanying saucer with marshmallows.

# Champagne Cocktail

### Ingredients

**Glass:** 140mL champagne flute

**Mixers:** 1 sugar cube
6 drops of Angostura bitters
15mL cognac or brandy
top up with champagne

### Method

In the flute, soak sugar cube in Angostura bitters, before adding brandy, then top with champagne.

**Garnish:** A strawberry.

# Cherries Jubilee

## Ingredients

**Glass:** 140mL cocktail glass

**Mixers:** 30mL cherry advocaat
30mL white crème de cacao
15mL Malibu
40mL cream
15mL milk

## Method

Shake with ice and strain.

**Garnish:** Grated chocolate and cherry and coconut shaving on side of glass.

**Comments:** Created by Leah Johns and won first place in Seagram's National Liqueur Championships, Hobart, Tasmania in 1990.

# Chiquita

## Ingredients

**Glass:**   285mL footed hi-ball glass

**Mixers:**  45mL vodka
          10mL banana liqueur
          10mL lime juice
          half a sliced banana
          pinch of sugar

## Method

Blend with ice and pour. Top with bitter lemon.

**Garnish:** Banana slices.

# Chivas Manhattan

### Ingredients
**Glass:** 90mL cocktail glass
**Mixers:** 30mL Chivas Regal Scotch whisky
15mL dry vermouth
15mL sweet vermouth
dash of Grand Mariner
piece of orange zest

### Method
Place ice cubes in glass, pour in Chivas Regal, dry and sweet vermouth and a dash of Grand Marnier. Stir thoroughly and strain into another chilled glass. Slice a piece of orange peel, set fire to the squeezed zest and place in the glass and enjoy.

**Garnish:** None.

**Comments:** An interesting change to a "traditional" Manhattan cocktail.

# Chivas Royal

## Ingredients

**Glass:** 140mL champagne flute

**Mixers:** 30mL Chivas Regal Scotch whisky

1 dash apple schnapps

ginger ale

## Method

Half fill a chilled champagne flute with crushed ice. Pour in Chivas Regal, add apple schnapps (or clear apple juice if preferred). Top up with ginger ale.

**Garnish:** Place a slice of green apple into the drink and serve.

**Comments:** A drink fit for a king.

# Cointreau Caipirinha

## Ingredients
**Glass:** 170mL old fashioned
**Mixers:** 30mL Cointreau
¼ fresh lime or lemon
crushed ice

## Method
Cut lime into pieces and place in glass. Extract juice by using the Cointreau pestle, fill glass with crushed ice and add Cointreau and mini pestle. Stir.

**Comments:** The pestle is a new Cointreau product which assists in the initial extraction of the lime or lemon juice.

**Garnish:** Lime wedge.

# Daiquiri

## Ingredients

**Glass:** 140mL champagne saucer

**Mixers:** 45mL rum
30mL lemon juice
15mL sugar syrup
½ egg white, optional

## Method

Shake with ice and strain.

**Garnish:** Lemon slice or lemon spiral.

**Comments:** Most Australian cocktail bars do not use egg white, however it definitely enhances the daiquiri's appearance. Ideal for large parties as batches can be stored ready for instant use. Mango, when in season, is very popular. When mixing a pure fruit daiquiri, it is best to use an electric blender and blend well with ice, then strain into a champagne saucer.

# Death In The Afternoon

**Ingredients**

**Glass:**  140mL champagne flute
**Mixers:** 15mL pernod
champagne to top

**Method**
Build, no ice.

**Garnish:** None.

**Comments:** Ernest Hemingway's favourite cocktail.
A bubbly occasion deserves this fully imported French
aphrodisiac mixer.

# Depth Charge

## Ingredients

**Glass:** 500mL schooner beer glass
20mL liqueur glass

**Mixers:** 400mL beer
20mL Drambuie*

## Method

Build, no ice. Fill glass with beer 3–5 centimetres below
the glass rim. Toast by touching liqueur glasses filled with
Drambuie before sliding into the beer glass.

**Garnish:** None.

**Comments:** You'll be amazed that the Drambuie remains in
the liqueur glass due to its higher density.

*Drambuie may be substituted with Lochan Ora.

# Dizzy Blonde

## Ingredients

**Glass:** 285mL hi-ball glass

**Mixers:** 60mL advocaat
30mL pernod
top up with lemonade

## Method

Shake over ice and pour then top up with lemonade.

**Garnish:** An orange slice and cherry.

# Double Jeopardy

## Ingredients

**Glass:** 285mL hi-ball glass

**Mixers:** 45mL Frangelico
45mL black Sambuca
scoop of vanilla ice cream
top up with milk

## Method

Blend with ice and stir.

**Garnish:** Scooper spoon (long teaspoon) and straws.

**Comments:** Take a chance on this cocktail. Remember you can't be tried for the same crime twice. Great in winter by an open fire.

# Dubonnet Cocktail

**Ingredients**

**Glass:**   125mL cocktail glass, chilled

**Mixers:**  30mL Dubonnet
15mL gin
1 dash orange bitters

**Method**

Build over ice.

**Garnish:** A lemon twist.

# El Burro

## Ingredients

**Glass:** 285mL fancy cocktail glass

**Mixers:** 15mL Kahlúa
15mL rum
30mL coconut cream
30mL cream
½ banana

## Method

Blend with ice and strain.

**Garnish:** Banana and mint leaves.

**Comments:** A full and thick style of cocktail, very popular at the moment. Definitely an afternoon cocktail.

# Evergreen

## Ingredients

**Glass:** 90mL cocktail glass

**Mixers:** 15mL dry vermouth
30mL gin
15mL melon liqueur
1½ teaspoons blue curaçao

## Method

Stir the first three ingredients of this pre-dinner cocktail over ice and strain into cocktail glass. Then drop the blue curaçao creating a visible layer.

**Garnish:** Red cherry on lip of glass

**Comments:** A poignant tasting cocktail consumed in summer.

# Fallen Angel (Australian Version)

## Ingredients
**Glass:** 285mL hi-ball glass
**Mixers:** 20mL advocaat
20mL cherry brandy
top up with lemonade

## Method
Build over ice and stir.

**Garnish:** Red cherry or strawberry. Serve with straws.

**Comments:** Although requiring individual taste bud approval, ensure advocaat and cherry Brandy are mixed thoroughly before topping up with lemonade. A **"Ruptured Rooster"** doesn't require the ingredients to be mixed.

# Fluffy Duck (No. 1)

## Ingredients

**Glass:** 285mL hi-ball glass

**Mixers:** 30mL rum
30mL advocaat
top up with lemonade
cream, floated

## Method

Build over ice.

**Garnish:** Orange slice and a red cherry. Serve with straws.

**Comments:** Most cocktail bars shake ingredients with cream before topping up with lemonade. When using a post mix gun, squirt the lemonade directly into the middle of the liquid surface instead of spraying against the back of the glass. This gives a billowing cloud effect.

# Fluffy Duck (No. 2)

## Ingredients

**Glass:**   140mL champagne saucer

**Mixers:** 30mL rum
30mL advocaat
30mL orange juice
30mL cream

## Method

Shake with ice and strain.

**Garnish:** Orange slice and a red cherry.

**Comments:** An after-dinner variation of the popular Fluffy Duck cocktail. A smoother and shorter drink.

# Frappe

## Ingredients
**Glass:** 90mL cocktail glass
**Mixers:** 30mL of preferred liqueur
(e.g. green crème de menthe)

## Method
Build over crushed ice.

**Garnish:** Two short straws.

**Comments:** Spoon the required quantity of crushed ice into the glass. Create spectacular rainbow effects with small quantities of liqueurs. Green crème de menthe is highly recommended because it acts as a breath freshener after dessert.

# Freddy-Fud-Pucker

## Ingredients

**Glass:** 285mL footed hi-ball glass
**Mixers:** 30mL tequila
120mL orange juice
15mL Galliano, floated

## Method

Build over ice.

**Garnish:** Orange slice and red cherry. Serve with straws.

**Comments:** Fantastic when drinking with friends – each participant after drinking half the cocktail says very quickly, 3 times, "Freddy Fud Puckers Fud any Puck". The first to be caught out is obliged to buy the next round. Be sure to mind your p's and f's when ordering.

# French Fantasy

## Ingredients

**Glass:** 140mL cocktail glass

**Mixers:** 30mL crème de Grand Marnier
30mL vodka
15mL Tia Maria
30mL pineapple juice
30mL orange juice

## Method

Shake with ice and strain.

**Garnish:** Banana slice and red cherry.

**Comments:** Crème de Grand Marnier is similar to Bailey's. This cocktail is really smooth and easy to drink.

# Geisha

## Ingredients

**Glass:**   140mL tulip champagne glass

**Mixers:**   30mL bourbon
30mL sake
10mL lemon juice
10mL sugar syrup

## Method

Shake over ice and strain.

**Garnish:** A red cherry.

# Georgia Peach

## Ingredients

**Glass:**  285mL hi-ball glass
**Mixers:** 30mL Bacardi
30mL peach liqueur
90mL cranberry juice

## Method

Build over ice and pour.

**Garnish:** A peach slice.

# Gibson

## Ingredients
**Glass:** 125mL cocktail glass
**Mixers:** 60mL gin
      10mL dry vermouth

## Method
Shake over ice and strain.

**Garnish:** One cocktail onion.

# Gimlet

## Ingredients

**Glass:** 175mL prism rocks glass

**Mixers:** 60mL gin
30mL lime juice

## Method

Shake over ice and pour, then add cubed ice.

**Garnish:** Two cocktail onions on toothpicks sunk in glass.

# God Daughter

## Ingredients

**Glass:** 140mL champagne saucer

**Mixers:** 30mL Sambuca
30mL Amaretto di Saronno
30mL cream
1 teaspoon grenadine

## Method

Shake with ice and strain.

**Garnish:** Flaked chocolate, strawberry and mint.

**Comments:** Ideal cocktail after Italian food.

# God Father

## Ingredients

**Glass:** 170mL old-fashioned spirit glass

**Mixers:** 30mL Scotch whisky
30mL Amaretto di Saronno

## Method

Build over ice.

**Garnish:** None.

**Comments:** To be drunk as either a pre-dinner drink or a nightcap. The guiding hand of Amaretto tempers the boldness of the Scotch.

# Golden Cadillac

## Ingredients

**Glass:** 140mL cocktail glass

**Mixers:** 30mL Galliano
30mL white crème de cacao
30mL cream

## Method

Shake with ice and strain.

**Garnish:** Red cherry or strawberry

**Comments:** The distilled cocoa beans will take you for the ride of your life. Cruise through this cocktail in luxurious style. Essential for all cocktail parties. Anywhere, anytime.

# Golden Dream

## Ingredients

**Glass:** 140mL cocktail glass

**Mixers:** 30mL Galliano
20mL Cointreau*
20mL orange juice
20mL cream

## Method

Shake with ice and strain.

**Garnish:** Red cherry on a toothpick on side of glass.

**Comments:** Chilled orange juice tarts the Galliano and freezes the Cointreau leaving a creamy tangy lining from your throat to your toes. Cointreau may be replaced with triple sec.

# Gomango

## Ingredients

**Glass:** 400mL hurricane glass

**Mixers:** 15mL triple sec
15mL white crème de cacao
15mL cherry advocaat
15mL orange juice
15mL cream
1 cheek of fresh mango

## Method

Blend with ice.

**Garnish:** Butterfly a strawberry on side of glass.

**Comments:** Created by Con Pandelakia, winner of 1991 Australian Title.

# Grasshopper

## Ingredients

**Glass:** 140mL champagne saucer

**Mixers:** 30mL crème de menthe
30mL white crème de cacao
30mL cream

## Method

Shake with ice and strain.

**Garnish:** 2 red cherries slit on the side of the glass.

**Comments:** Jump right into this very popular after dinner cocktail. Some people prefer dark crème de cacao instead of white crème de cacao. Shake until smooth.

# G.R.B.

## Ingredients

**Glass:** 90mL cocktail glass

**Mixers:** 30mL Galliano
10mL grenadine
30mL dark rum

## Method

Build over ice.

**Garnish:** Float a mint leaf.

**Comments:** Anyone who stalls gets a double-hit-round. The mint permeates the rum leaving a refreshingly sweet aftertaste. Use your imagination to name this acronym!

# Greek God

## Ingredients

**Glass:** whisky shot

**Mixers:** 15mL ouzo
15mL pernod

## Method

Pour in order then shoot.

**Garnish:** None.

# Green with Envy

### Ingredients

**Glass:** 200mL hurricane glass

**Mixers:** 30mL ouzo
30mL blue curaçao
120mL pineapple juice

### Method

Shake with ice and pour.

**Garnish:** Pineapple spear with leaves and cherry. Serve with straws.

**Comments:** An afternoon cocktail. The aniseed in Ouzo chills the pineapple juice. As they say...jealousy's fragrant a curse, envy is worse.

# Harvey Wallbanger

### Ingredients

**Glass:**   285mL hi-ball glass

**Mixers:**  45mL vodka
125mL orange juice
15mL Galliano, floated

### Method

Build over ice.

**Garnish:** Orange slice and cherry. Swizzle stick and straws.

**Comments:** Hawaiian bartenders will tell you a visiting Irishman called Harvey pin-balled down the corridor to hotel room after a night out. Hence, he was known as "Harvey Wallbanger".

# Hawaiian Punch

## Ingredients

**Glass:** 285mL hi-ball glass

**Mixers:** 20mL Southern Comfort
20mL Amaretto
15mL vodka
40mL pineapple juice
40mL orange juice
20mL lime juice
20mL grenadine

## Method

Shake over ice and pour, then add grenadine.

**Garnish:** Orange slice and a red cherry.

# Hurricane

## Ingredients

**Glass:**   200mL hurricane glass

**Mixers:**  30mL Bacardi
             30mL orange juice
             15mL lime cordial
             45mL lemon juice
             45mL sugar syrup
             top with 15mL Bacardi Gold

## Method

Shake with ice and pour. Serve with straws.

**Garnish:** Orange slice and cherry.

# Irish Coffee

## Ingredients

**Glass:** 250mL Irish Coffee glass

**Mixers:** 30mL Bailey's Irish Cream
1 teaspoon brown sugar
top up with hot black coffee
float fresh whipped cream

## Method

Build, no ice.

**Garnish:** Chocolate flake optional.

**Comments:** The most widely drunk liqueur coffee which verifies its approval amongst coffee lovers. Tullamore Dew and Jameson's are most popular Irish whiskies. Other liqueur coffees are: **French – brandy, English – gin, Russian – vodka, American – bourbon, Calypso – dark rum, Jamaican – Tia Maria, Parisienne – Grand Marnier, Mexican – Kahlúa, Monks – Benedictine, Scottish – Scotch Whisky, Canadian – rye.**

# Japanese Slipper

## Ingredients

**Glass:**   90mL cocktail glass
**Mixers:** 30mL melon liqueur
        30mL Cointreau
        30mL lemon juice

## Method

Shake with ice and strain.

**Garnish:** Slice of lemon on side of glass.

**Comments:** Simple to prepare and the habit preferences of consumers has ensured this cocktail will remain one most often requested. Pouring 1 teaspoon of grenadine upon completion of the cocktail gives a marvellous visual effect and sweetens the sour element.

# Jelly Bean

## Ingredients

**Glass:** 285mL hi-ball glass

**Mixers:** 30mL ouzo
15mL blue curaçao
15mL grenadine
top up with lemonade

## Method

Build over ice.

**Garnish:** Swizzle stick and straws. Red cherry dropped into glass.

**Comments:** A cool liquid confectionery. Dropping blue curaçao and grenadine into the cocktail after presenting to the customer gives a swirling lollipop effect. Regularly drunk without the blue curaçao.

# Kamikaze

## Ingredients
**Glass:** 140mL cocktail glass
**Mixers:** 30mL vodka
30mL Cointreau
30mL fresh lemon juice
1 teaspoon lime cordial

## Method
Shake with ice and strain.

**Garnish:** Red cocktail onion on a toothpick in the glass.

**Comments:** Maintain freshness for larger volumes by adding stained egg white. Mix in a jug and keep refrigerated. For the hyper active. Cointreau may be replaced with triple sec.

# Kelly's Comfort

## Ingredients

**Glass:** 285mL hi-ball glass

**Mixers:** 30mL Southern Comfort
30mL Bailey's Irish Cream
30mL milk
4 strawberries
15mL sugar syrup

## Method

Blend over ice and pour.

**Garnish:** A strawberry.

# K.G.B.

### Ingredients

**Glass:** 170mL old-fashioned spirit glass

**Mixers:** 30mL Kahlúa
30mL Grand Marnier
30mL Bailey's Irish Cream

### Method

Build over ice.

**Garnish:** None.

**Comments:** The first letter of each of the ingredients give this cocktail its name. A late night party drink.

# Kick in the Balls

## Ingredients

**Glass:** 140mL champagne saucer

**Mixers:** 30mL rum
30mL orange juice
30mL melon liqueur
30mL cream
15mL coconut cream

## Method

Shake with ice and strain.

**Garnish:** Two melon balls previously marinated in the rum.

**Comments:** Float melon balls. Using a toothpick, eat both balls together and you'll be sure to feel a "Kick in the Balls". Refrigerate melon balls to preserve their freshness.

# Kir

### Ingredients
**Glass:** 140mL wine goblet
**Mixers:** 15mL cassis liqueur
top up with dry white wine

### Method
Build, no ice.

**Garnish:** None.

**Comments:** A superb pre-dinner drink. Use cold wines. Do not spoil the drink by using more than 15mL of cassis liqueur. To make a **"Kir Imperial"** substitute 5mL grenadine for 15mL cassis. **"Kir Royale"** is served in a 140mL champagne flute with only 5mL cassis liqueur and topped with the best champagne available. Always remember, the better the champagne, the better the drink. Serve chilled.

**Hint:** Sprinkle a thumb pinch of sugar to produce fizzy bubbles from the champagne.

# Lady M

### Ingredients
**Glass:** 285mL hurricane glass
**Mixers:** 45mL Frangelico
45m melon liqueur
2 scoops vanilla ice cream

### Method
Blend for more than 20 seconds to thoroughly mix
ingredients.

**Garnish:** Strawberry on side of glass sprinkled with grated
chocolate.

**Comments:** Be adventurous and try various flavoured
ice creams.

# Lamborghini

## Ingredients
**Glass:** 90mL cocktail glass
**Mixers:** 20mL crème de café
20mL Cointreau
20mL Sambuca
cold fresh cream

## Method
Layer ingredients in the above order using a spoon, then float fresh cream.

**Garnish:** Grated chocolate flakes.

**Comments:** As the name suggests, speed is the object of this cocktail. You may like to try drinking each layered ingredient through a straw at a quickening speed; similar to changing the gears in a Lamborgini.

# Lamborghini (Flaming)

## Ingredients

**Glass:**   4–6 tall Dutch cordial glasses

**Mixers:**  20mL Kahlúa per cocktail
20mL Cointreau per cocktail
20mL Sambuca per cocktail
cold fresh cream

## Method

Heat and build.

**Garnish:** Grated chocolate flake.

**Comments:** Warm alcoholic ingredients in a saucepan.
Be sure to simmer flame to avoid scorching Kahlúa. Stand
glasses in a row and allow flame to burn for 10–15 seconds.
Pour cold cream into a spoon and float onto the cocktail to
extinguish flame. The nightclub version replaces Sambuca for
green chartreuse as it is distinct in colour, easier to layer and
also flamed.

# Leprechaun

## Ingredients

**Glass:**   200mL old-fashioned spirit glass

**Mixers:**  60mL Irish whisky
top up with tonic water

## Method

Build over ice.

**Garnish:** A lime slice dropped into the glass.

# Lights of Havana

## Ingredients

**Glass:** 285mL hi-ball glass

**Mixers:** 60mL soda water
45mL Malibu
30mL Midori
60mL orange juice
60mL pineapple juice

## Method

Shake over ice and pour.

**Garnish:** A straw and a lime wheel.

# Lip Sip Suck

## Ingredients

**Glass:**  whisky shot

**Mixers:**  30mL tequila
lemon in quarters or slices
salt

## Method

Pour tequila into glass. On the flat piece of skin between the base of your thumb and index finger, place a pinch of salt. Place a quarter of the lemon on the bar. Lick the salt off your hand, shoot the tequila and then suck the lemon in quick succession.

**Garnish:** None.

# Long Island Iced Tea

### Ingredients

**Glass:** 285mL hi-ball glass

**Mixers:** 30mL vodka
30mL lemon juice
30mL tequila
30mL sugar syrup

30mL white rum
30mL Cointreau
dash of cola

### Method

Build over Ice.

**Garnish:** Lemon twist and mint leaves. Serve with straws.

**Comments:** The tea-coloured cola is splashed into the cocktail making it slightly unsuitable for a "tea party". Many variations are concocted using different white spirits. It is strongly recommended that you consume no more than one.

# Louisiana Lullaby

## Ingredients
**Glass:**   90mL cocktail glass
**Mixers:**  30mL dark rum
        10mL Dubonnet
        1 teaspoon Grand Marnier

## Method
Shake over ice and strain.

**Garnish:** A twist of lemon.

# Madame Butterfly

### Ingredients

**Glass:** 140mL margarita glass

**Mixers:** **Shake 1**

30mL Passoa (or ½ passionfruit)
15mL melon liqueur
15mL white crème de cacao
30mL pineapple juice

**Shake 2**

30mL cream
15mL melon liqueur

### Method

This cocktail requires two shakers. In one hand, shake the first four ingredients over ice and strain. In the other hand, shake melon liqueur and cream, then layer.

**Garnish:** Strawberry and Butterfly.

**Comments:** An innovative award-winning cocktail.

# Mai-Tai

## Ingredients

**Glass:** 285mL hi-ball glass

**Mixers:** 30mL rum
30mL lemon juice
15mL Amaretto di Saronno
30mL sugar syrup

15mL dark rum
½ fresh lime juiced
30mL orange curaçao

## Method

Shake with ice and pour.

**Garnish:** Pineapple spear, mint leaves, tropical flowers if possible (e.g. Singapore orchid), lime shell. Serve with straws.

**Comments:** A well-known rum-based, refreshing, tropical cocktail. Grenadine is often added to redden a glowing effect while the rum may be floated on top when served without straws. Rum lovers drink their Mai Tais this way. It can also be built into a tall glass and stirred with the pineapple spear.

# Malibu Magic

## Ingredients

**Glass:** 285mL hurricane glass

**Mixers:** 30mL Malibu*
30mL strawberry liqueur
30mL orange juice
3–4 fresh strawberries
60mL cream

## Method

Blend with ice and pour.

**Garnish:** A single strawberry and twisted orange peel.

**Comments:** Shake to the wonders of Californian dreaming.
15mL of Cointreau may be added for that magic moment.
*Malibu may be substituted with coconut liqueur.

# Manhattan

## Ingredients
**Glass:**  90mL cocktail glass
**Mixers:**  30mL bourbon
         15mL rosso vermouth
         dash Angostura bitters

## Method
Stir over ice and strain.

**Garnish:** A red cherry on toothpick in glass.

**Comments:** A pre dinner cocktail. Replace rosso vermouth with dry vermouth, add a twist of lemon and you have instantly mixed a dry Manhattan. Rye whisky may be substituted for bourbon.

# Margarita

## Ingredients

**Glass:** 140mL margarita glass, salt-rimmed

**Mixers:** 30mL tequila
30mL lemon juice
15mL Cointreau
½ egg white, optional

## Method

Shake with ice and strain.

**Garnish:** Lemon wheel on edge of glass.

**Comments:** Margaritas can be 'shaken' or 'frozen' – a professional bartender will always ask which method is preferred. A **"Frozen Margarita"** contains ⅓ of the blender full of ice. Add water if the mix becomes gluggy.

# Martini

## Ingredients

**Glass:** 90mL cocktail glass
**Mixers:** 45mL gin
20mL dry vermouth

## Method

Stir over ice and strain.

**Garnish:** Lemon twist or olive on toothpick in the glass.

**Comments:** The classically sophisticated black-tie cocktail. Always stirred, however, when shaken it is known as a **"Bradford"**. An olive garnish retains the gin sting whereas a lemon twist makes the cocktail smoother.

**Note:** A "dry martini" has less vermouth.

# Midori Avalanche

## Ingredients

**Glass:** 285mL hurricane glass

**Mixers:** 30mL blue curaçao
30mL Midori
15mL triple sec
60mL pineapple juice

## Method

Pour blue curaçao into glass. Blend other ingredients with ice and pour.

**Garnish:** Triangle of pineapple on side of glass.

**Comments:** This deep sea cocktail can be found at poolside bars around Australia. Be sure to use plenty of ice to quench a hot dry thirst.

# Mint Julep

## Ingredients

**Glass:** 285mL Tom Collins glass

**Mixers:** 60mL bourbon
1 teaspoon sugar
2–3 dashes cold water or soda water
8 sprigs of fresh mint
crushed or shaved ice

## Method

Muddle sugar, water and 5 mint sprigs in a glass. Pour into thoroughly frosted glass and pack with ice. Add bourbon and mix (with a chopping motion using a long-handled bar spoon).

**Garnish:** Remaining mint and serve with a straw.

**Comments:** Tear mint leaves slightly before sugaring for greater aroma.

# Monkey Gland

## Ingredients

**Glass:** 125mL cocktail glass

**Mixers:** 30mL gin

10mL apple juice

1 teaspoon Parfait Amour

1 teaspoon grenadine

## Method

Shake with ice and strain.

**Garnish:** Plastic monkey.

**Variation:** Substitute 20mL pernod for the Parfait Amour and grenadine.

# Montmartre

### Ingredients
**Glass:** 90mL cocktail glass
**Mixers:** 10mL Cointreau
10mL Cointreau
30mL gin
10mL sweet vermouth

### Method
Coat glass with Cointreau then pour gin and sweet vermouth over ice.

**Garnish:** Red cherry on side of glass.

**Comments:** From the world-renowned painters courtyard next to the Sacré Coeur overlooking Paris.

# Moscow Mule

## Ingredients

**Glass:**  285mL hi-ball glass

**Mixers:**  30mL vodka

15mL lime cordial

top up with ginger beer

## Method

Build over ice.

**Garnish:** Slice of lemon and mint. Straws and swizzle stick.

**Comments:** A long, cool, refreshing cocktail. It tastes a lot better if the juice of half a lime is squeezed into the cocktail in place of the lime cordial.

# Mount Temple

## Ingredients

**Glass:**  90mL cocktail glass

**Mixers:** 30mL Kahlúa
           30mL tequila
           30mL coconut liqueur

## Method

Build over ice.

**Garnish:** Dollop of cream in centre of glass.

**Comments:** Love is a temple and you'll love this higher ground.

# Negroni

## Ingredients
**Glass:**  90mL cocktail glass
**Mixers:**  20mL Campari
         20mL sweet vermouth
         10mL gin

## Method
Shake with ice and strain.

**Garnish:** A twist of lemon and orange peel.

# Old Fashioned – Scotch

## Ingredients

**Glass:**   285mL old-fashioned spirit glass

**Mixers:**  30mL Scotch whisky
splash Angostura bitters
sugar cube
soda water

## Method

Splash bitters evenly over the sugar cube before adding ice, Scotch and topping up with soda.

**Garnish:** ½ slice of orange and lemon and a cherry.
A swizzle stick may be used.

**Comments:** A soothing 'knocking-off' drink after 5pm. Ensure cherries are dry. If cherries are moist, the juice may taint the flavour, thereby marring the appearance. Scotch, bourbon or rye whisky may be served in the **"Old Fashioned"** way.

# Ole

## Ingredients

**Glass:**  90mL cocktail glass

**Mixers:**  30mL tequila
30mL banana liqueur
10mL blue curaçao

## Method

Stir the tequila and banana liqueur gently over ice to avoid 'bruising' and strain into the glass, then drop blue curaçao.

**Garnish:** Lemon wheel.

**Comments:** 1988 World Cocktail Championship winner. It not only looks good but is great to drink. Easy to make if you're in a hurry.

# Orgasm

### Ingredients
**Glass:** 200mL old-fashioned spirit glass
**Mixers:** 20mL Bailey's Irish Cream
20mL Cointreau

### Method
Build over ice.

**Garnish:** Strawberry or cherries, optional.

**Comments:** Probably the most widely drunk cocktail in Australia and very popular with the ladies. A **"Multiple Orgasm"** is made with the addition of 30mL of fresh cream or milk. A **"Screaming Multiple Orgasm"** has the addition of 15mL Galliano along with 30mL fresh cream or milk.

# Pago Pago

## Ingredients

**Glass:** 250mL old-fashioned spirit glass

**Mixers:** 30mL Bacardi Gold Rum
10mL lime juice
10mL pineapple juice
1 teaspoon green Chartreuse
1 teaspoon Cointreau

## Method

Shake with ice and strain over 3 cubes of ice.

**Garnish:** A pineapple wedge and a cherry.

# Palm Sundae

## Ingredients

**Glass:**  285mL hurricane glass

**Mixers:** 45mL peach liqueur
30mL coconut liqueur
15mL banana liqueur
60mL tropical fruit juice
3 fresh strawberries

## Method

Blend with ice and pour.

**Garnish:** Orange wedge, pineapple leaves and maraschino cherry.

**Comments:** Peach liqueur is exquisite in this specially designed cocktail. The succulent peach flavour is another member in the new generation of natural tropical fruit cocktails.

# Picasso

## Ingredients

**Glass:** 90mL cocktail glass

**Mixers:** 30mL cognac
10mL Dubonnet
10mL lime juice
15mL sugar syrup

## Method

Shake over ice and strain.

**Garnish:** An orange twist.

# Pimm's No. 1 Cup

## Ingredients

**Glass:**   285mL hi-ball glass

**Mixers:**  30-45mL Pimm's No. 1 Cup

top up with either lemonade or dry ginger
or equal parts of both

## Method

Build over ice.

**Garnish:** Orange and lemon slice, cherries, cucumber skin, swizzle stick and straws.

**Comments:** A slice of orange can detract from the sweet aftertaste. Slicing the inside of the cucumber skin allows the small drops to keep the drink chilled. Originally 6 Pimm's numbers were commonly consumed, today there are only two. Pimm's No.1 – gin base, Pimm's No. 2 – vodka base. Often referred to as the **"Fruit Cocktail Cocktail"**.

# Pina Colada

## Ingredients

**Glass:** 285mL hi-ball glass

**Mixers:** 30mL dark rum
30mL coconut cream
30mL sugar syrup
125mL unsweetened pineapple juice

## Method

Shake with ice and pour.

**Garnish:** Pineapple wedge, three leaves and a cherry. Straws and swizzle stick.

**Comments:** Another tropical Hawaiian cocktail, which is distinguished by including coconut cream. Unfortunately, it is not normally stocked by Australian bars. If temporarily unavailable, coconut liqueur will suffice. Cream is optional for a richer blend.

# Pink Panther

## Ingredients

**Glass:** 140mL champagne saucer

**Mixers:** 22mL bourbon
30mL vodka
15mL Malibu
40mL cream
dash of grenadine

## Method

Shake with ice and strain

**Garnish:** Cherry and mint.

**Comments:** Leap out of a 'pink fit' with one of the first coconut cocktails made in Australia. For the intrepid.

# Planters Punch

### Ingredients

**Glass:** 150mL cocktail glass

**Mixers:** 30mL dark rum
30mL lemon or lime juice
60mL orange juice
1 teaspoon grenadine

### Method

Build over ice then add grenadine.

**Garnish:** Fruit slices.

# Polish Sidecar

## Ingredients

**Glass:** 90mL cocktail glass

**Mixers:** 20mL gin
20mL lemon juice
10mL raspberry liqueur

## Method

Shake gin and lemon juice with ice and pour then float raspberry liqueur.

**Garnish:** Raspberries.

# Polynesia

## Ingredients

**Glass:** 140mL tulip champagne glass

**Mixers:** 30mL white rum
30mL melon liqueur
10mL lime juice
½ egg white

## Method

Blend with ice and pour.

**Garnish:** Banana.

# Prairie Oyster

## Ingredients

**Glass:** 90mL cocktail glass

**Mixers:** 30mL brandy
salt and pepper
Worcestershire sauce
Tabasco sauce
1 egg yolk

## Method

Build, no ice.

**Garnish:** None.

**Comments:** The spices relieve a sore head and the brandy replenishes lost energy. Brandy may be replaced with any spirit of your choice, however cold vodka is medicinally soothing. Best before breakfast.

# Pretty Woman

## Ingredients

**Glass:**   285mL hurricane glass

**Mixers:** **Blender 1**          **Blender 2**

       30mL melon liqueur    30mL strawberry liqueur

       30mL Malibu             3–4 strawberries

## Method

Blend with ice in two separate blenders and pour.

**Garnish:** Strawberry and umbrella on side of glass.

**Comments:** Remember to tilt the glass when pouring the two sets of ingredients into the glass. Choosing a long glass will assist you. Very alcoholic as there is no juice. A kaleidoscope of colour for you to enjoy.

# P.S. I Love You

### Ingredients

**Glass:**   150mL champagne saucer

**Mixers:**  30mL Amaretto
          30mL Kahlúa
          30mL Bailey's Irish Cream
          1 teaspoon grenadine

### Method

Build over ice and stir.

**Garnish:** Sprinkled nutmeg.

# Quebec

## Ingredients

**Glass:**   125mL cocktail glass

**Mixers:**  30mL Canadian Club whisky
10mL dry vermouth
10mL Amer Picon
10mL maraschino liqueur

## Method

Shake over ice and strain.

**Garnish:** A cocktail onion.

**Comments:** Amer Picon is a French brand of bitters that derives much of its flavour from gentian root and oranges. 3mL Angostura bitters may be substituted.

# Raffles Singapore Sling

### Ingredients
**Glass:** 285mL hi-ball glass
**Mixers:** 30mL gin
30mL orange juice
30mL cherry brandy liqueur
30mL lime juice
30mL pineapple juice
15mL triple sec
15mL Benedictine
dash Angostura bitters

### Method
Shake with ice and pour.

**Garnish:** Orange slice, mint, a cherry, swizzle stick and straws.

**Comments:** This recipe is the original Singapore version, with its fruit juices it tastes totally different from some gin slings commonly served in bars.

# Red Eye

## Ingredients
**Glass:**  300mL cocktail glass
**Mixers:**  200mL beer
           90mL tomato juice

## Method
Build no ice.

**Garnish:** None.

# Rocket Fuel

## Ingredients

**Glass:** 200mL fancy cocktail glass

**Mixers:** 15mL rum
15mL dry gin
15mL vodka
60mL lemonade
15mL tequila

## Method

Build over ice.

**Garnish:** Swizzle stick.

**Comments:** This cocktail secured it's bar fame when Australia's rock legend Jimmy Barnes sang about "sitting on the beach drinking Rocket Fuel...oh yeah!"

# Rusty Nail

### Ingredients
**Glass:**   200mL old-fashioned spirit glass
**Mixers:**  30mL Scotch whisky
         30mL Drambuie

### Method
Build over ice.

**Garnish:** Lemon twist (optional).

**Comments:** A traditional pillow softener for refined
gentlemen. Hailing from the highlands of Scotland, Drambuie
will raise your spirit above the centre of the world. Lemon will
diffuse the bite of the Scotch. Watch your step when ordering!

# Salty Dog

### Ingredients
**Glass:**  285mL hi-ball glass – salt-rimmed
**Mixers:** 45mL vodka
top up with grapefruit juice

### Method
Build over ice.

**Garnish:** Swizzle stick, straws optional.

**Comments:** Slowly re-emerging as the long cool cocktail it was renowned for in its heyday. Unfortunately, a limited number of bars stock grapefruit juice, which restricts availability. But as the saying goes "Every dog has his day". Straws are generally unnecessary, drink the cocktail from the salt rim.

# Sangria

## Ingredients
**Glass:**   170mL wine glass
**Mixers:**  20mL Cointreau
        20mL brandy
        20mL Bacardi
        orange, lime, lemon and strawberry pieces
        20mL sugar syrup
        80mL red wine

## Method
Pour in order. Thinly slice orange, lemon and lime, chop strawberries and place in bowl. Pour in sugar syrup and allow to stand for several hours. Add red wine.

**Garnish:** None.

# Satin Pillow

### Ingredients

**Glass:** 140mL cocktail glass

**Mixers:** 1 teaspoon strawberry liqueur
10mL Cointreau
15mL Frangelico
15mL Tia Maria
20mL pineapple juice
20mL cream

### Method

Blend with ice and pour.

**Garnish:** Cut a strawberry in half and place on side of glass then swirl cream over strawberry halves.

**Comments:** The very piquant taste is as smooth as satin bed linen.

# Screwdriver

## Ingredients

**Glass:**  200mL old-fashioned spirit glass

**Mixers:** 45mL vodka
      45mL orange juice

## Method

Build over ice.

**Garnish:** Orange twist or spiral.

**Comments:** A frequently requested basic spirit mixed drink. Subtle at any time of day. The original recipe contains equal measurements of vodka and orange juice. **A Comfortable Screw** is made with 30mL vodka, 15mL Southern Comfort and topped with orange juice. **A Slow Comfortable Screw** has the addition of 15mL sloe gin. **A Long Slow Comfortable Screw** is a longer drink served in a 285mL hi-ball glass. **A Long Slow Comfortable Screw Up Against A Wall** has the addition of 15mL Galliano floated.

# Scorpion

### Ingredients

**Glass:** 140mL cocktail glass

**Mixers:** 15mL dark rum
15mL cognac
15mL Sambuca
15mL orgeat syrup
45mL orange juice
15mL lemon juice

### Method

Blend with ice.

**Garnish:** A lime wheel with cherry.

**Comments:** From the trading capital of the Middle East is where this perilous animal and cocktail comes from! Remember they have a sting in their tail. Orgeat is an almond-flavoured non-alcoholic syrup. Amaretto may be used as a substitute.

# Sex on the Beach

## Ingredients

**Glass:**   200mL fancy cocktail glass

**Mixers:**  15mL Kahlúa
           30mL Malibu
           30mL pineapple liqueur
           60mL cream

## Method

Shake with ice and strain.

**Garnish:** Pineapple wedge on side of glass.

**Comments:** A most enjoyable cocktail when you feel mischievous.

# Shanghai Punch

### Ingredients
**Glass:**   360mL fancy hi-ball glass
**Mixers:**  30mL cognac
30mL dark rum
45mL orange juice
20mL Cointreau
20mL lemon juice
almond extract
fresh tea
grated orange and lemon peel
cinnamon stick

### Method
Boil tea and add ingredients then stir.

**Garnish:** None.

# Sicilian Kiss

### Ingredients
**Glass:** 150mL old-fashioned spirit glass
**Mixers:** 30mL Southern Comfort
30mL Amaretto

### Method
Build with ice.

**Garnish:** None.

# Sidecar

## Ingredients

**Glass:** 90mL cocktail glass

**Mixers:** 30mL brandy
20mL Cointreau*
20mL lemon juice

## Method

Shake with ice and strain.

**Garnish:** Lemon twist optional.

**Comments:** A zappy pre-dinner cocktail. The lemon juice purifies the brandy and ferments the Cointreau. Too much lemon juice will leave an acidic aftertaste.

*Cointreau may be substituted with triple sec.

# Snowball

## Ingredients

**Glass:** 285mL hi-ball glass

**Mixers:** 30mL advocaat
top up with lemonade
dash of lime cordial
cream, optional

## Method

Build over ice.

**Garnish:** Red cherry. Swizzle sticks and straws.

**Comments:** Place ice in the glass after mixing the advocaat with lemonade and before floating the cream on top. The pressure of a post mix gun will create the desired 'snowball' effect.

# South Pacific

## Ingredients

**Glass:**  285mL hi-ball glass

**Mixers:**  30mL dry gin

15mL Galliano

top with lemonade

15mL blue curaçao

## Method

Build over ice, then add the blue curaçao last.

**Garnish:** Lemon slice and cherry, swizzle stick and straws.

**Comments:** Australia's first gold medal-winning cocktail. Created by Gary Revell, and won the World Cocktail Championships in Yugoslavia in 1979.

# Southern Peach

### Ingredients

**Glass:** 140mL martini glass

**Mixers:** 30mL Cointreau
15mL brandy
15mL cherry brandy liqueur
15mL pineapple juice
15mL lemon juice

### Method

Shake with ice and strain.

**Garnish:** Butterfly a strawberry, place on side of glass, twirl cream over strawberry and sprinkle flaked chocolate.

**Comments:** A magical cocktail that can be 'fluffed' up by adding egg white.

# Splice

## Ingredients
**Glass:**   200mL hurricane glass
**Mixers:**   30mL Midori
          15mL Galliano
          15mL coconut liqueur
          30mL pineapple juice
          30mL cream

## Method
Blend with ice and pour.

**Garnish:** Pineapple wedge and leaves on side of glass.

**Comments:** Enjoyed in Australia for several years. The smooth, well blended flavour has ensured this cocktails ever increasing admiration.

# Spritzer

## Ingredients

**Glass:** 170mL wine goblet

**Mixers:** dry white wine, chilled
soda water

## Method

Build, no ice.

**Garnish:** None.

**Comments:** "Wet the whistle" with a responsible alcoholic alternative. Ladies prefer the soda dilution although you may be asked for lemonade.

## Stars & Stripes

### Ingredients

**Glass:** 285mL fancy cocktail glass

**Mixers:** 10mL blue curaçao

| **Blender 1** | **Blender 2** |
|---|---|
| 30mL Southern Comfort | 30mL strawberry liqueur |
| 30mL Frangelico | 3–4 strawberries |

### Method

Pour blue curaçao into glass. Blend other ingredients with ice in 2 separate blenders and pour.

**Garnish:** Sprinkle grated chocolate flakes over top and add a strawberry and USA flag to side of glass.

**Comments:** Remember to tilt the glass when pouring the two sets of ingredients. A refreshingly super-powered alcoholic cocktail without juice.

# Stinger

### Ingredients

**Glass:** 90mL cocktail glass

**Mixers:** 45mL brandy
10mL white crème de menthe

### Method

Stir over ice and strain.

**Garnish:** None.

**Comments:** The distinct minty aroma of white crème de menthe pervades this prefect pre-dinner cocktail. The brandy delivers the sting!

# Strawberry Blonde

## Ingredients

**Glass:** 285mL hi-ball glass

**Mixers:** 30mL dark crème de cacao
top up with cola
fresh cream, floated
splash of grenadine

## Method

Build over ice.

**Garnish:** A red cherry. Swizzle sticks and straws.

**Comments:** Tasting this cocktail will reveal the secret why 'blondes have more fun'. Placing ice in the glass after mixing the crème de cacao with cola will support the floating cream on top. A dessert cocktail. Ideal on a blind date.

# Summer Breeze

### Ingredients
**Glass:** 285mL fancy cocktail glass
**Mixers:** 60mL Peachtree liqueur
15mL rum
15mL mango liqueur
15mL gin
60mL pineapple juice
60mL orange juice
1 fresh mango
1 fresh peach

### Method
Blend with ice and pour.

**Garnish:** Half an orange slice and orange peel twist.

**Comments:** A glorious cocktail slurped on the Great Barrier Reef. With temperature hot and humidity high, this is often the only summer breeze available in the afternoon.

# Sunken Treasure

### Ingredients
**Glass:**  90mL cocktail glass
**Mixers:**  30mL gin
15mL peach liqueur
champagne to top up
apricot conserve

### Method
Stir over ice, strain and top up with champagne.

**Garnish:** Place a teaspoon of apricot conserve in the bottom of glass and then push a strawberry into conserve.

**Comments:** It is always pleasing to include innovative cocktail garnishes. 1989 Australian National Cocktail winner

# Swedish Snowball

## Ingredients

**Glass:** 200mL old-fashioned spirit glass

**Mixers:** 30mL advocaat
15mL lemon juice
top up with soda water

## Method

Build over ice then top up with soda.

**Garnish:** A lemon slice.

# Sweet Lady Jane

### Ingredients

**Glass:** 140mL champagne saucer

**Mixers:** 15mL Grand Marnier
15mL orange juice
15mL Cointreau
15mL coconut cream
30mL strawberry liqueur
30mL fresh cream

### Method

Shake with ice and strain.

**Garnish:** Strawberry, mint and chocolate flakes.

**Comments:** An orange-glazed cocktail gorgeously presented with chocolate flakes that swirl in the coconut and strawberry liqueurs.

# Sweet Martini

### Ingredients
**Glass:** 90mL cocktail glass
**Mixers:** 45mL dry gin
20mL rosso vermouth

### Method
Stir over ice and strain.

**Garnish:** Red cherry on toothpick in glass.

**Comments:** Sister to the **"Dry Martini"**, the sweeter vermouth overwhelms the gin sting. A pre-dinner cocktail which can be stirred and strained either: **"On The Rocks"** – served in a standard spirit glass over ice or **"Straight Up"** – served in a 90mL cocktail glass over ice.

# Tequila Slammer

### Ingredients
**Glass:** 170mL old-fashioned spirit glass
**Mixers:** 30mL tequila
       60mL dry ginger ale

### Method
Build, no ice.

**Garnish:** None.

**Comments:** A one hit wonder - holding a coaster over the entire rim, rotate the glass clockwise on the bar 4–5 times. Lift and 'slam' the base of the glass down onto the bar, then skol in one shot. The carbonated mixer fizzes the tequila when slammed. Usually bartenders splash only 5–10mL of dry ginger ale to aid the quick drinking process.

# Tequila Sunrise

### Ingredients
**Glass:**   285mL hi-ball glass
**Mixers:** 30mL tequila
          1 teaspoon grenadine
          top up with orange juice

### Method
Build over ice.

**Garnish:** Orange wheel, a red cherry. Swizzle stick and straws.

**Comments:** Sipping this long cool cocktail at sunrise or sunset is magnificent. To obtain the cleanest visual effect, drop grenadine down the inside of the glass, after topping up with orange juice. Dropping grenadine in the middle creates a fallout effect, detracting from the presentation of the cocktail. Best served with chilled, freshly squeezed orange juice.

# The Dik Hewett

### Ingredients

**Glass:**   140mL cocktail glass

**Mixers:**  30mL Jack Daniel's Old No. 7
30mL cognac
30mL Benedictine
glass of water (on the side)

### Method

Shake with ice and strain.

**Garnish:** None.

**Comments:** The late arrival cocktail. Sure to test, sure to please.

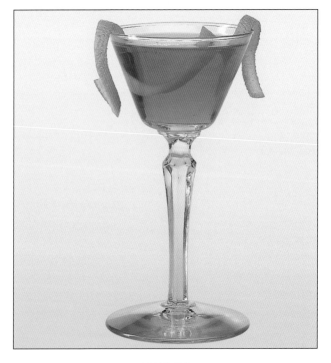

# T.N.T.

### Ingredients

**Glass:** 90mL cocktail glass

**Mixers:** 45mL brandy
20mL orange liqueur
dash of Pernod
dash of Angostura bitters

### Method

Stir over ice and strain.

**Garnish:** Orange twist.

**Comments:** A powder keg, really a cocktail to liven up any party. Drink in moderation, as this one can really cause a "bang".

# Toblerone

## Ingredients

**Glass:**   140mL cocktail glass

**Mixers:**   1 teaspoon Bailey's Irish Cream
15mL Kahlúa
15mL white crème de cacao
30mL Frangelico
60mL cream
½ teaspoon honey

## Method

Blend with ice and pour.

**Garnish:**  Sprinkle almond flakes and nutmeg over top. To create a special effect drag a cotton strand over completed cocktail.

**Comments:** A favourite at Melbourne's Collins Street exclusive 5-star cocktail bars. Accompanying chocolates make this cocktail bliss before the theatre.

# Tom Collins

### Ingredients

**Glass:** 140mL champagne saucer
**Mixers:** 60mL lemon juice
 60mL gin
 soda water

### Method

Put cracked ice, lemon juice, and gin in a glass. Fill with soda water and stir.

**Garnish:** Serve with a slice of lemon and cherry.

**Comments:** Brandy, bourbon, rum or any whisky can be used instead of gin, the Collins is named after the liquor used, eg. Rum Collins.

# Trader Vic's Rum Fizz

## Ingredients

**Glass:** 140mL tulip champagne glass

**Mixers:** 30mL dark rum
30mL lemon juice
10mL sugar
15mL creaming soda
1 raw egg

## Method

Shake over ice and pour.

**Garnish:** An orange spiral.

**Comments:** From the range of cocktails for which the internationally renowned cocktail-bar proprietor has become recognised.

# Tropical Itch

## Ingredients

**Glass:** 400mL hurricane glass

**Mixers:** 45mL rum
45mL bourbon
juice of half lime
dash Angostura bitters
top up with pineapple juice and passionfruit
30mL dark rum, floated

## Method

Build over ice.

**Garnish:** Pineapple spear, mint and cherry plus wooden backscratcher and straws.

**Comments:** When you're troubled with an itching-tickling throat, delight in this spectacularly garnished fruity cocktail. A proven thirst-quenching recipe after sunbaking. The name is derived from the inclusion of the backscratcher.

# Voodoo Child

### Ingredients

**Glass:**   90mL cocktail glass

**Mixers:**  15mL melon liqueur
15mL black Sambuca
15mL Bailey's Irish Cream
15mL Tia Maria
15mL cream

### Method

Layer melon liqueur on black Sambuca in glass. Shake other ingredients with ice and strain.

**Garnish:** Green and black jelly babies on a skewer, then place across top of glass.

**Comments:** Scare yourself with this novel cocktail. It's a fun-filled cocktail guaranteed to lift any spell.

# Whisky Sour

### Ingredients
**Glass:** 140mL wine glass
**Mixers:** 45mL Scotch whisky
30mL lemon juice
15mL sugar syrup
½ egg white

### Method
Shake with ice and strain.

**Garnish:** Red cherry at bottom of glass and slice of lemon on side.

**Comment:** A quaint appetiser before dinner. Shake vigorously so the egg white rises to a frothy head after straining. Some people prefer a 140mL cocktail glass.

# White Lady

### Ingredients
**Glass:** 90mL cocktail glass
**Mixers:** 30mL dry gin
15mL lemon juice
15mL sugar syrup
½ egg white

### Method
Shake with ice and strain.

**Garnish:** Twist of lemon.

**Comments:** A traditional pre-dinner cocktail. Pure yet tasty, change to either: "Blue Lady" – substitute blue curaçao for sugar syrup. "Pink Lady" – substitute grenadine for sugar syrup and add cream.

## Widow's Kiss

### Ingredients

**Glass:** 90mL cocktail glass

**Mixers:** 30mL apple brandy
10mL Benedictine
10mL yellow chartreuse
1 teaspoon Angostura bitters

### Method

Shake over ice and strain.

**Garnish:** A floating strawberry.

# Woodstock

## Ingredients

**Glass:** 140mL old-fashioned spirit glass
sugar rimmed with maple syrup

**Mixers:** 30mL gin
10mL lemon juice
10mL maple syrup
2 dashes Angostura bitters

## Method

Shake over ice and strain then add cubed ice.

**Garnish:** None.

# X.T.C.

### Ingredients
**Glass:** 90mL cocktail glass
**Mixers:** 30mL Tia Maria
30mL strawberry liqueur
30mL cream

### Method
Shake with ice and strain.

**Garnish:** Butterfly strawberry placed on side of glass, twirl thickened cream over strawberry and sprinkle over flaked chocolate.

**Comments:** X-rated, tall and cute! Enjoy a truly enjoyable ecstasy before you dance all night long.

# Zombie

## Ingredients

**Glass:** 285mL fancy cocktail glass

**Mixers:** 40mL Bacardi     15mL lime or lemon juice
30mL dark rum     30mL apricot brandy
30mL light rum     1 teaspoon sugar syrup
30mL pineapple juice

## Method

Shake with ice and pour.

**Garnish:** Pineapple spear and leaves, mint leaves and cherry, swizzle stick and straws.

**Comments:** A well-known Hawaiian cocktail. Resurrect yourself with this supernatural rum-a-thon cocktail. It is usually the last recipe on cocktail lists.

# After Eight

## Ingredients

**Glass:** cordial (Embassy)

**Mixers:** 10mL Kahlúa
10mL green crème de menthe
10mL Bailey's Irish Cream
1 teaspoon Southern Comfort

## Method

Pour in order.

**Technique:** Shoot.

**Comments:** A peppermint surprise.

# Atomic Bomb

## Ingredients

**Glass:**  tall Dutch cordial

**Mixers:**  20mL Tia Maria

15mL gin

10mL cream

## Method

Layer in order, then float cream.

**Technique:** Shoot.

**Comments:** A strategic 'one shooter weapon', this drink explodes down the unsuspecting throat. Delicious in emergencies! Gin may be replaced with Cointreau, or triple sec.

# B&B Shooter

### Ingredients

**Glass:** cordial (Lexington)

**Mixers:** 15mL cognac or brandy
15mL Benedictine

### Method

Pour in order.

**Technique:** Shoot.

**Comments:** For mature drinkers! Grandpa can turn up the pace of his medication. The shooter is quick and smooth, the traditional B&B cocktail is normally served in a brandy balloon.

# Banana Split

## Ingredients

**Glass:**  tall Dutch cordial

**Mixers:**  15mL Kahlúa
15mL Lena banana liqueur
10mL strawberry liqueur
whipped cream

## Method

Layer in order and top with whipped cream.

**Technique:** Shoot.

**Comments:** Let this one slip down sweetly, with a super strawberry aftertaste.

# Bee Sting

### Ingredients
**Glass:** cordial (Embassy)
**Mixers:** 20mL tequila
10mL yellow chartreuse

### Method
Layer in order, then light.

**Technique:** Straw shoot while flaming.

**Comments:** Ouch! The yellow Chartreuse attacks your throat with a numbing, pleasurable pain, as tequila buzzes you back to the party. Drink quickly so the straw won't melt!

# Black Nuts

## Ingredients
**Glass:** cordial (Embassy)
**Mixers:** 15mL black sambuca
          15mL Frangelico

## Method
Layer in order.

**Technique:** Shoot.

**Comments:** A wonderful "nutty" flavour, with a real anise touch.

# Black Widow

## Ingredients
**Glass:** cordial (Embassy)

**Mixers:** 10mL strawberry liqueur
10mL black Sambuca
10mL cream

## Method
Layer in order.

**Technique:** Shoot.

**Comments:** Watch this one, the spider will get you quickly.

## Blood Bath

### Ingredients

**Glass:** whisky shot

**Mixers:** 10mL sweet vermouth
15mL strawberry liqueur
20mL tequila

### Method

Pour in order then layer the tequila.

**Technique:** Shoot.

**Comments:** Cherry grins and rosy cheeks characterise the after effects of this blood thirsty experience. Only issued after midnight and before dawn.

# Blow Job

## Ingredients

**Glass:**   cordial (Lexington)

**Mixers:**   30mL Kahlúa
        15mL Bailey's Irish Cream

## Method

Layer in order and shoot.

**Technique:** Shoot.

**Comments:** A light, minty confectionery flavour and creamy texture provide a mouthful for those who indulge. Twist this to a **"Rattlesnake"** by adding green Chartreuse.

# Brain Damage

### Ingredients
**Glass:** cordial (Embassy)
**Mixers:** 10mL coconut liqueur
10mL Parfait Amour
1 teaspoon Advocaat

### Method
Layer the Parfait Amour and coconut liqueur, then pour the Advocaat.

**Technique:** Shoot.

**Comments:** *Separation induces restless nights. Advocaat intervenes to mould the senses.*

# Brave Bull

### Ingredients
**Glass:** whisky shot
**Mixers:** 30mL crème de café
15mL tequila

### Method
Layer in order.

**Technique:** Shoot.

**Comments:** One of my favourites for late night revellers, will help resist fatigue and maintain stamina. Add ouzo and a "TKO" is punched out.

# Candy Cane

## Ingredients

**Glass:** tall Dutch cordial

**Mixers:** 15mL grenadine
15mL crème de menthe
15mL vodka

## Method

Layer in order.

**Technique:** Shoot.

**Comments:** A real candy flavour, with a touch of menthol.

# Chastity Belt

## Ingredients

**Glass:**   tall Dutch cordial

**Mixers:**  15mL Tia Maria
15mL Frangelico
10mL Bailey's Irish Cream
1 teaspoon cream

## Method

Layer in order, then float the cream.

**Technique:** Shoot.

**Comments:** Morality implores you not to succumb to the super-sweet delicacies of drinking's perversity.

# Chilli Shot

### Ingredients
**Glass:** whisky shot
**Mixers:** 45mL vodka
slice of red chilli

### Method
Pour.

**Technique:** Shoot.

**Comments:** Feeling mischievous? Refrigerate the vodka with one red chilli (or 3–5 drops of Tabasco sauce) for 24 hours before serving.

# Chocolate Nougat

## Ingredients

**Glass:** cordial (Embassy)

**Mixers:** 10mL Frangelico
10mL Benedictine
10mL Bailey's Irish Cream

## Method

Pour in order then layer the Bailey's Irish Cream.

**Technique:** Shoot.

**Comments:** A swirling pleasure zone of flowing Bailey's Irish Cream, above the finest Benedictine and based on voluptuous hazelnuts, accentuating the flavour of chocolate.

# Coathanger

## Ingredients

**Glass:** cordial (Embassy)
**Mixers:** 15mL Cointreau*
10mL tequila
1 teaspoon grenadine
drop of milk

## Method

Layer tequila onto the Cointreau, dash of grenadine then drop in the milk.

**Technique:** Shoot, then cup hand entirely over the rim, insert straw between fingers into the glass and inhale fumes.

**Comments:** A euphoric experience, quietly stunning your senses.

*Cointreau may be replaced with triple sec.

# Courting Penelope

## Ingredients

**Glass:** cordial (Embassy)

**Mixers:** 20mL cognac
10mL Grand Marnier

## Method

Pour in order.

**Technique:** Shoot.

**Comments:** A distinctive acquired taste is needed for two inseparable liquors!

# Dark Sunset

### Ingredients
**Glass:** tall Dutch cordial
**Mixers:** 20mL dark crème de cacao
20mL Malibu

### Method
Layer in order.

**Technique:** Shoot.

**Comments:** This tropical paradise reflects sunset, beaches and the ripe coconuts of Malibu.

# Devil's Handbrake

## Ingredients

**Glass:** tall Dutch cordial

**Mixers:** 15mL banana liqueur
15mL mango liqueur
15mL cherry brandy

## Method

Layer in order.

**Technique:** Shoot

**Comments:** *A magnificent bounty of fruit infiltrated by the devil. Exquisite after a swim.*

# Dirty Orgasm

## Ingredients

**Glass:**   tall Dutch cordial

**Mixers:**   15mL triple sec
          15mL Galliano
          15mL Bailey's Irish Cream

## Method

Layer in order.

**Technique:** Shoot.

**Comments:** The Irish frolic between the world's two best lovers, Italian Galliano and French Cointreau. Also known as a **"Screaming Orgasm"**. Drambuie may replace the Galliano.

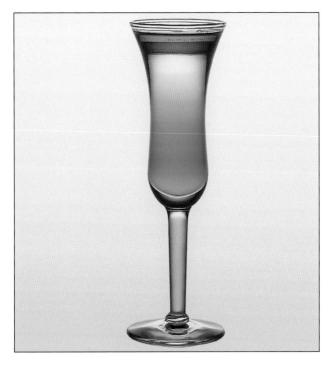

# Double Date

### Ingredients
**Glass:**  tall Dutch cordial
**Mixers:** 15mL melon liqueur
    15mL white crème de menthe
    15mL Benedictine

### Method
Layer in order.

**Technique:** Tandem.

**Comments:** Soothing crème de menthe restrains the passion of DOM and melon. For romantics.

# Face Off

## Ingredients
**Glass:** tall Dutch cordial
**Mixers:** 10mL grenadine
15mL crème de menthe
10mL Parfait Amour
10mL Sambuca

## Method
Layer in order.

**Technique:** Shoot.

**Comments:** Too many of these will certainly cause a loss of face.

# Fizzy Rush

## Ingredients

**Glass:**  tall Dutch cordial

**Mixers:**  1 teaspoon white crème de menthe

10mL apricot brandy

30mL champagne

## Method

Pour in order.

**Technique:** Shoot.

**Comments:** Bubbles of refreshing apricot guaranteed to get up your nose.

# Flaming Lamborghini Shooter

**Ingredients**

**Glass:** cordial (Embassy)

**Mixers:** 10mL crème de café
10mL Galliano
10mL green Chartreuse

**Method**

Layer in order, then light.

**Technique:** Shoot while flaming.

**Comments:** Get the party in motion. Essential for birthday celebrants.

# Flaming Lover

## Ingredients

**Glass:**   cordial (Embassy)

**Mixers:**  15mL Sambuca
             15mL triple sec

## Method

Pour triple sec over lit Sambuca.

**Technique:** Straw shoot while flaming.

**Comments:** The triple sec softens the flame for inexperienced drinkers of flaming shooters.

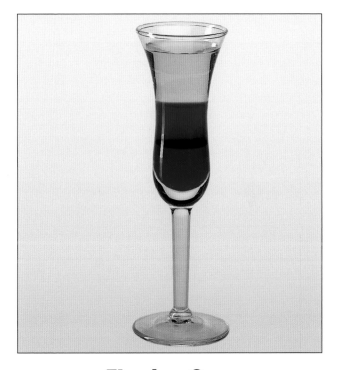

# Flaming Orgy

## Ingredients

**Glass:** tall Dutch cordial

**Mixers:** 10mL grenadine
10mL crème de menthe
15mL brandy
10mL tequila

## Method

Layer in order.

**Technique:** Straw shoot while flaming.

**Comments:** Another of the potent flaming shooters. Don't get your lips too close to this one.

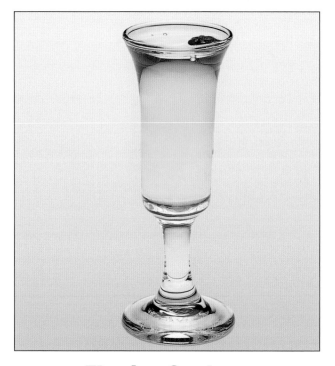

# Flaming Sambuca

## Ingredients

**Glass:** cordial (Embassy)

**Mixers:** 30mL Sambuca
3 coffee beans

## Method

Pour Sambuca, float coffee beans and light.

**Technique:** Shoot after flame extinguished.

**Comments:** Provides relief from the cold winter. The other way we do it, is to pour Sambuca into a wine glass then light. Cup your hand entirely over the rim while it flames, creating suction. Shake the glass, place under your nose, take your hand from the glass to inhale the fumes, then shoot!

# Freddie Fud Pucker Shooter

## Ingredients

**Glass:** cordial (Lexington)

**Mixers:** 20mL Galliano
10mL tequila
1 teaspoon orange curaçao

## Method

Layer tequila onto Galliano then drop in orange curaçao.

**Technique:** Shoot.

**Comments:** Known to induce dancing on bars and at beach parties, be sure to mind you 'p's and 'f's when ordering.

# Fruit Tingle

### Ingredients

**Glass:**  cordial (Embassy)

**Mixers:**  10mL blue curaçao
15mL mango liqueur
1 teaspoon lemon juice

### Method

Layer in order, optional to stir.

**Technique:** Shoot.

**Comments:** Tangy and piquant. Melon liqueur may be substituted for mango liqueur.

## Galliano Hot Shot

### Ingredients

**Glass:**  Galliano shot glass
**Mixers:**  15mL Galliano
30mL black coffee
1 teaspoon cream

### Method

Top Galliano with black coffee, then float cream.

**Technique:** Shoot.

**Comments:** When in a hurry, a great way to enjoy a liqueur coffee.

# Golden Cadillac Shooter

### Ingredients

**Glass:** tall Dutch cordial

**Mixers:** 15mL white crème de cacao
20mL Galliano
10mL cream

### Method

Layer Galliano and white crème de cacao, then float cream.

**Technique:** Shoot.

**Comments:** Comfort in style is what the distilled cocoa beans give golden Galliano - a real dazzler! The traditional Golden Cadillac cocktail has a larger volume, is shaken over ice and served in a 140mL champagne saucer.

# Grand Slam

## Ingredients

**Glass:**  cordial (Embassy)

**Mixers:**  10mL Lena banana liqueur
10mL Bailey's Irish Cream
10mL Grand Marnier

## Method

Pour in order, then stir.

**Technique:** Shoot.

# Green Slime

### Ingredients

**Glass:**  whisky shot

**Mixers:**  20mL melon liqueur
15mL vodka
1 teaspoon egg white

### Method

Pour in order, then stir.

**Technique:** Shoot.

**Comments:** Add more egg white for greater slime.
Melon will keep the taste buds occupied, vodka dilutes the
egg white.

# Half Nelson

### Ingredients

**Glass:** whisky shot

**Mixers:** 15mL crème de menthe
10mL strawberry liqueur
20mL Grand Marnier

### Method

Layer in order.

**Technique:** Shoot.

**Comments:** The referee is unable to break the grip of strawberry locking its minty green opponent into an immovable position. For the temporarily incapacitated.

# Harbour Lights

## Ingredients

**Glass:**  cordial (Lexington)

**Mixers:**  10mL Kahlúa
10mL Sambuca
10mL green Chartreuse

## Method

Layer in order.

**Technique:** Straw shoot.

**Comments:** Glittering reflections sparkle on the harbour beside a candlelight dinner. Substitute yellow Chartreuse if preferred.

# Hard On

## Ingredients

**Glass:** tall Dutch cordial

**Mixers:** 20mL crème de café
15mL banana liqueur
10mL cream

## Method

Layer liqueurs in order, then float the cream.

**Technique:** Shoot.

**Comments:** The first shooter to float cream, voted the most popular shooter.

# Hellraiser

**Ingredients**

**Glass:**   whisky shot

**Mixers:**  15mL strawberry liqueur
15mL melon liqueur
15mL black Sambuca

**Method**

Layer in order.

**Technique:** Shoot.

**Comments:** A hell of a drink!

# High and Dry

## Ingredients

**Glass:**   cordial (Embassy)

**Mixers:**  10mL bianco vermouth

         15mL tequila

         1 teaspoon dry vermouth

## Method

Pour in order, then stir.

**Technique:** Shoot.

**Comments:** Disguise the mischief of tequila with dry vermouth. Best served chilled.

# Inkahlúarable

## Ingredients

**Glass:**   cordial (Embassy)

**Mixers:**  10mL Kahlúa
             10mL triple sec
             10mL Grand Marnier

## Method

Layer in order.

**Technique:** Shoot.

**Comments:** Terminal illness can be momentarily postponed with this Kahlúa-based antidote.

# Irish Flag

## Ingredients

**Glass:** cordial (Lexington)

**Mixers:** 10mL green crème de menthe
10mL Bailey's Irish Cream
10mL brandy

## Method

Layer in order.

**Technique:** Shoot.

**Comments:** A stroll through verdant pastures. Brandy may be replaced with Tullamore Dew-an Old Irish whisky.

# Italian Stallion

## Ingredients

**Glass:** cordial (Lexington)

**Mixers:** 15mL banana liqueur
15mL Galliano
1 teaspoon cream

## Method

Pour Galliano onto banana liqueur, then float cream. Optional to stir.

**Technique:** Shoot.

**Comments:** A creamy banana ride you won't forget.

# Japanese Slipper Shooter

### Ingredients

**Glass:** tall Dutch cordial

**Mixers:** 20mL melon liqueur
15mL triple sec*
10mL lemon juice

### Method

Layer triple sec onto the melon liqueur then float the lemon juice. Optional to stir.

**Technique:** Shoot.

**Comments:** Elegant and refreshing. Precision is required with measurements. Use to revive failing confidence and replenish that special feeling.

*Cointreau may be substituted for triple sec.

# Jawbreaker

## Ingredients
**Glass:**  whisky shot
**Mixers:**  45mL apricot brandy
 4–5 drops Tabasco sauce

## Method
Pour apricot brandy then drop Tabasco sauce.

**Technique:** Shoot.

**Comments:** Grit your teeth after this shot, then slowly open your mouth.

# Jellyfish

## Ingredients

**Glass:** cordial (Lexington)

**Mixers:** 10mL blue curaçao
10mL Romana Sambuca
10mL Bailey's Irish Cream
2 dashes of grenadine

## Method

Layer in order and then pour grenadine.

**Technique:** Shoot.

**Comments:** Watch out for sting at the end of this slippery shooter.

# Jumping Jack Flash

### Ingredients
**Glass:** whisky shot
**Mixers:** 15mL Tia Maria
15mL rum
15mL Jack Daniel's

### Method
Layer in order.

**Technique:** Shoot.

**Comments:** Thrill seeking Jack Daniel's and his accomplices await this opportunity to shudder your soul.

# Jumping Mexican

### Ingredients
**Glass:** whisky shot
**Mixers:** 20mL crème de café
20mL bourbon

### Method
Layer in order.

**Technique:** Shoot.

**Comments:** Jump into Mexico's favourite pastime and bounce back into the party. For those keen on the Mexican Hat Dance.

# Kamikaze Shooter

### Ingredients

**Glass:** whisky shot

**Mixers:** 20mL vodka
15mL Cointreau
10mL lemon juice

### Method

Layer the Cointreau onto vodka, float the lemon juice, then optional to stir.

**Technique:** Shoot.

**Comments:** Maintain freshness for large volumes by adding strained egg white. Mix in a jug and keep refrigerated. The traditional Kamikaze cocktail has the additional of Lime cordial, it is shaken over ice, strained and then served in a 140mL cocktail glass. Triple sec may be substituted for Cointreau.

# K.G.B. Shooter

## Ingredients

**Glass:** cordial (Lexington)
**Mixers:** 10mL Kahlúa
10mL Grand Marnier
10mL Bailey's Irish Cream

## Method

Layer in order.

**Technique:** Shoot.

**Comments:** Grand Marnier adds an orange twist to the Kahlúa and Bailey's Irish Cream. The traditional K.G.B. cocktail is built over ice with greater volume of ingredients.
It is normally served in a 140mL old-fashioned spirit glass.

# Kool Aid

## Ingredients

**Glass:** cordial (Lexington)

**Mixers:** 10mL melon liqueur
15mL Amaretto di Saroono
10mL vodka

## Method

Layer in order.

**Technique:** Shoot.

**Comments:** A familiar mix with various names. Amaretto's caramel lacing prevents overheating.

# Lady Throat Killer

### Ingredients

**Glass:**   tall Dutch cordial

**Mixers:** 20mL crème de café
15mL melon liqueur
10mL Frangelico

### Method

Layer in order.

**Technique:** Shoot.

**Comments:** This superb mixture offers an exquisite aftertaste.
One of my favourite shooters.

# Lambada

### Ingredients
**Glass:** whisky shot
**Mixers:** 15mL mango liqueur
15mL black Sambuca
15mL tequila

### Method
Layer in order.

**Technique:** Shoot.

**Comments:** Wiggle your way to the bar and order a shooter with the latest liqueur, black Sambuca. Both the dance and the shooter will excite.

# Laser Beam

## Ingredients

**Glass:** tall Dutch cordial

**Mixers:** 25mL Galliano
15mL tequila

## Method

Layer in order.

**Technique:** Shoot.

**Comments:** Your palate is illuminated on this celestial journey!

# Lick Sip Suck

### Ingredients

**Glass:**   whisky shot

**Mixers:** 30mL tequila
            lemon in quarters or slices
            salt

### Method

Pour tequila into glass.

**Technique:** On the flat piece of skin between the base of your thumb and index finger, place a pinch of salt. Place a quarter of the lemon by you on the bar. Lick the salt off your hand, shoot the tequila and then suck the lemon in quick succession.

# Marc's Rainbow

### Ingredients

**Glass:**   whisky shot

**Mixers:**  10mL crème de café
10mL melon liqueur
10mL Malibu
10mL banana liqueur
10mL Galliano
10mL Grand Marnier

### Method

Layer in order.

**Technique:** Shoot.

**Comments:** One of Melbourne's best shooter recipes.
Discover the pot of gold at the end of the rainbow.

# Margarita Shooter

### Ingredients

**Glass:**   whisky shot

**Mixers:**   15mL Cointreau*
15mL tequila
10mL lemon juice
1 teaspoon lime juice

### Method

Layer tequila onto Cointreau, float lemon juice then add a dash of the lime juice.

**Technique:** Shoot.

**Comments:** Everyone should take this plunge. Lemon and lime neutralise the acid. This shooter is similar to the traditional margarita cocktail, which is of greater volume, shaken over ice and served in a salt-rimmed champagne saucer.

*Triple sec may be substituted for Cointreau.

# Martian Hard On

## Ingredients

**Glass:** tall Dutch cordial

**Mixers:** 15mL dark crème de cacao
15mL melon liqueur
15mL Bailey's Irish Cream

## Method

Layer in order.

**Technique:** Shoot.

**Comments:** When you are a little green about the facts of life.

# Melon Splice

### Ingredients

**Glass:**   tall Dutch cordial

**Mixers:**  15mL melon liqueur
15mL Galliano
15mL coconut liqueur

### Method

Layer in order.

**Technique:** Shoot.

**Comments:** Synonymous with Sunday strolls and ice cream.
Flakes of ice may be sprinkled to chill.

# Mexican Flag

## Ingredients

**Glass:**  tall Dutch cordial

**Mixers:** 15mL grenadine
15mL crème de menthe
15mL tequila

## Method

Layer in order.

**Technique:** Shoot.

**Comments:** Try this "South of the Border" flag waver.

# Nude Bomb

## Ingredients

**Glass:** cordial (Embassy)

**Mixers:** 10mL Kahlúa
10mL banana liqueur
10mL Amaretto di Saronno

## Method

Layer in order.

**Technique:** Shoot.

**Comments:** Especially created for toga parties and skinny-dipping.

# Orgasm Shooter

**Ingredients**

**Glass:**   whisky shot

**Mixers:**  15mL Cointreau*
             15mL Bailey's Irish Cream

**Method**

Layer in order.

**Technique:** Shoot.

**Comments:** After the first one, you most certainly will want another. The shooter method is different to the traditional Orgasm cocktail, which is a longer drink, built over ice and served in a 210mL old-fashioned spirit glass.

*Triple sec may be substituted for Cointreau.

# Oyster Shooter

## Ingredients

**Glass:** cordial (Embassy)

**Mixers:** 10mL vodka
10mL tomato juice
1 teaspoon tomato sauce
Worcestershire sauce to taste
Tabasco sauce to taste
1 fresh oyster

## Method

Pour tomato juice onto the vodka, float the tomato sauce, dash Worcestershire and Tabasco sauces to taste and drop in oyster.

**Technique:** Shoot.

**Comments:** An early morning wake-up call, replenishing energy lost the night before. Also referred to as a **"Heart Starter"**.

# Passion Juice

## Ingredients

**Glass:** whisky shot

**Mixers:** 20mL orange curaçao
10mL cherry brandy
15mL freshly squeezed orange or lemon juice

## Method

Layer in order. Optional to stir.

**Technique:** Shoot.

**Comments:** A bitter-sweet lift by garnishing liqueur passion with juices.

# Peach Bay

## Ingredients

**Glass:**  tall Dutch cordial

**Mixers:**  25mL Peachtree schnapps
15m Pimm's No. 1 Cup
1 teaspoon green crème de menthe

## Method

Layer the Pimm's onto the Peachtree schnapps, then drop green crème de menthe.

**Technique:** Shoot.

**Comments:** Conjuring an image of uninhabited places, cool refreshing Pimm's is minted with green crème de menthe.

# Peachy Bum

## Ingredients

**Glass:** tall Dutch cordial

**Mixers:** 20mL mango liqueur
15mL Peachtree schnapps
10mL cream

## Method

Layer in order.

**Technique:** Shoot.

**Comments:** Delightfully enriched and mellowed by fresh cream.

# Pearl Necklace

## Ingredients
**Glass:** cordial (Embassy)

**Mixers:** 15mL melon liqueur
15mL Pimm's No. 1 Cup

## Method
Layer in order.

**Technique:** Shoot.

**Comments:** A dash of lemonade dilutes the zappy aftertaste.

# Perfect Match

### Ingredients
**Glass:** cordial (Lexington)
**Mixers:** 30mL Parfait Amour liqueur
30mL Malibu

### Method
Layer in order.

**Technique:** Shoot.

**Comments:** Parfait (perfect), Amour (love), proposes future happiness and togetherness under Malibu's exotic veil.

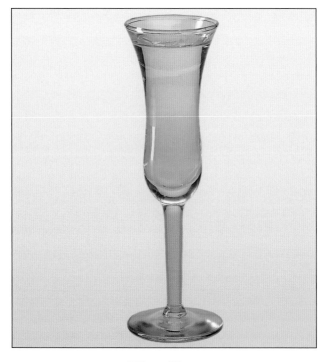

# Pipeline

## Ingredients
**Glass:** tall Dutch cordial
**Mixers:** 25mL tequila
15mL vodka

## Method
Layer in order.

**Technique:** Shoot.

**Comments:** Ride the wild surf in this pipeline.

# Pipsqueak

## Ingredients

**Glass:** cordial (Embassy)

**Mixers:** 20mL Frangelico
10mL vodka
1 teaspoon lemon juice

## Method

Layer in order, then stir.

**Technique:** Shoot.

**Comments:** Another favourite of mine. A quaint appetiser before dinner.

# Rabbit-Punch

## Ingredients

**Glass:**   whisky shot

**Mixers:**  10mL Campari
10mL dark crème de cacao
10mL Malibu
15mL Bailey's Irish Cream

## Method

Pour in order then layer Bailey's Irish Cream.

**Technique:** Shoot.

**Comments:** Bailey's Irish Cream assures credibility and its softness will subtly inflict a powerful jab to wake you up and keep you on the hop!

# Ready, Set, Go!

### Ingredients

**Glass:** tall Dutch cordial

**Mixers:** 15mL strawberry liqueur
15mL banana liqueur
15mL Midori

### Method

Layer in order.

**Technique:** Shoot.

# Red Indian

## Ingredients

**Glass:** cordial (Lexington)

**Mixers:** 10mL dark crème de cacao
10mL Peachtree schnapps
15mL Canadian Club

## Method

Layer in order.

**Technique:** Shoot.

**Comments:** Dark crème de cacao ripens the Peachtree to tantalise. Canadian Club takes the scalp!

# Rusty Nail

## Ingredients

**Glass:** cordial (Embassy)
**Mixers:** 15mL Scotch whisky
15mL Drambuie

## Method

Layer in order.

**Technique:** Shoot.

**Comments:** A pillow-softener, though this age-old blend will never cause fatigue. As a shooter, great as "one for the road". The traditional cocktail is normally built over ice, in a 210mL old-fashioned spirit glass.

# Ryan's Rush

## Ingredients

**Glass:**   cordial (Embassy)

**Mixers:**  10mL Kahlúa
10mL Bailey's Irish Cream
10mL dark rum

## Method

Layer in order.

**Technique:** Shoot.

**Comments:** An easy one. Don't be lulled by the pleasant taste, this one has a real kick.

# Screaming Death Shooter

**Ingredients**

**Glass:**   tall Dutch cordial

**Mixers:**   15m crème de café

15mL bourbon

10mL Benedictine

1 teaspoon dark rum

## Method

Layer in the above order. Lighting optional.

**Technique:** Shoot while flaming.

**Comments:** The pinnacle of endurance. Double layers of flammable fuel cushioned in ascending order by crème de café, bourbon and Benedictine, which sweetly numbs any pain. It's truth and dare.

# Screwdriver Shooter

### Ingredients
**Glass:**  whisky shot
**Mixers:**  15mL orange liqueur
          30mL vodka

### Method
Layer in order.

**Technique:** Shoot.

**Comments:** Add a dash of Peachtree schnapps and it's known as a **"Fuzzy Navel"**. The shooter mix departs from the traditional Screwdriver cocktail by the substitution of orange liqueur for orange juice. The cocktail is also built over ice in a 210mL old-fashioned spirit glass.

# Sex in the Snow

## Ingredients

**Glass:** cordial (Lexington)

**Mixers:** 10mL triple sec, chilled
10mL Malibu, chilled
10mL ouzo, chilled

## Method

Pour in order, then stir.

**Technique:** Straw shoot.

**Comments:** The sub-zero temperature of this combination is chillingly refreshing when drunk through a straw.

# Sherbert Burp

## Ingredients

**Glass:**   tall Dutch cordial

**Mixers:**  15mL strawberry liqueur
            30mL champagne

## Method

Pour strawberry liqueur then top up with champagne.

**Technique:** Shoot.

**Comments:** Change the colour of your burp with any flavoured liqueur. Even better, multicolour it!

# Sidecar Shooter

## Ingredients

**Glass:**   cordial (Lexington)

**Mixers:**   10mL brandy
15mL Cointreau*
10mL lemon juice

## Method

Layer Cointreau onto brandy, float lemon juice, then optional to stir.

**Technique:** Shoot.

**Comments:** This old-fashioned, lemon-barley refreshment, filtered through Cointreau and lightly tanned with brandy, restores your zest for life. A slightly different mix to the traditional Sidecar cocktail, which is shaken over ice and served in a 90mL cocktail glass.

*Cointreau may be substituted with triple sec.

# Silver Thread

## Ingredients

**Glass:** tall Dutch cordial

**Mixers:** 15mL crème de menthe
15mL banana liqueur
15mL Tia Maria

## Method

Layer in order.

**Technique:** Shoot or lick, sip and suck.

**Comments:** A great shooter to mend the fences. Try this one with the oldies.

# Slippery Nipple

### Ingredients
**Glass:**  cordial (Embassy)
**Mixers:**  20mL Sambuca
10mL Bailey's Irish Cream

### Method
Layer in order.

**Technique:** Shoot.

**Comments:** One of the originals, very well received.
Cream floated on the Bailey's becomes a **"Pregnant Slippery Nipple"**. Grand Marnier included makes a **"Slipadictome"**.

## Snake Bite

### Ingredients

**Glass:** cordial (Embassy)
**Mixers:** 20mL crème de café
10mL green Chartreuse

### Method

Layer in order, then light.

**Technique:** Straw shoot while flaming.

**Comments:** Score this shooter ten out of ten. Drink quickly or the straw will melt.

# Spanish Fly

### Ingredients

**Glass:** whisky shot

**Mixers:** 10mL bianco vermouth
15mL tequila
20mL whisky

### Method

Layer in order.

**Technique:** Tandem.

**Comments:** No, it's not what you're twinkling eye and devious smirk assumes...it's better. A guaranteed survival capsule, capable of producing fantasies beyond those Spain is famous for.

# Springbok

## Ingredients

**Glass:** cordial (Embassy)

**Mixers:** 15mL passionfruit syrup, or ½ passionfruit
10mL crème de menthe
1 teaspoon ouzo

## Method

Layer in order.

**Technique:** Shoot.

**Comments:** Named after the beautiful springbok of Africa, formerly a motif on the South African rugby jersey.

# Strawberry Cream

## Ingredients

**Glass:**   cordial (Embassy)

**Mixers:**  20mL strawberry liqueur
       10mL cream

## Method

Layer in order.

**Technique:** Shoot.

**Comments:** Begin your trip to the World of Shooters with this one. Cream acts as a buffer to entice the nervous and inexperienced. Strawberries calm what was needless concern.

## Suction Cup

### Ingredients

**Glass:**   cordial (Lexington)

**Mixers:**  20mL vodka
10mL melon liqueur
1 teaspoon blue curaçao

### Method

Layer the melon liqueur onto vodka, then pour blue curaçao.

**Technique:** Suction and straw shoot.

**Comments:** A supersonic vacuum results from this drinking method.

# Suitor

## Ingredients

**Glass:**   cordial (Lexington)

**Mixers:**  10mL Drambuie*
10mL Grand Marnier
10mL Bailey's Irish Cream
1 teaspoon milk

## Method

Pour in order.

**Technique:** Shoot.

**Comments:** The inclusion of milk coddles a cool moment, resettles anxieties when approaching the fairer sex, guaranteed to excite romance.

*Drambuie may be substituted with Lochan Ora.

# Sukiyaki

## Ingredients

**Glass:** cordial (Embassy)

**Mixers:** 10mL mango liqueur
10mL apricot brandy
10mL Malibu

## Method

Layer in order.

**Technique:** Shoot.

**Comments:** Essential starter for a superb Japanese banquet.

# Test Tube Baby

## Ingredients

**Glass:** tall Dutch cordial

**Mixers:** 30mL Grand Marnier
15mL ouzo
drop of Bailey's Irish Cream

## Method

Layer in order.

**Technique:** Shoot.

# The Day After

## Ingredients

**Glass:**  cordial (Embassy)
**Mixers:** 10mL Cointreau*
10mL tequila
5 drops blue curaçao
10mL green Chartreuse

## Method

Layer tequila onto Cointreau. Drop the blue curaçao, then layer green Chartreuse and light.

**Technique:** Shoot after flame extinguished.

**Comments:** An upside down day!

*Cointreau may be substituted with triple sec.

# T.K.O.

## Ingredients

**Glass:**   cordial (Embassy)

**Mixers:**  10mL Kahlúa

10mL tequila

10mL ouzo

## Method

Layer in order.

**Technique:** Shoot.

**Comments:** Don't fall with this T.K.O., drink it with pleasure, recover without pain.

# Tickled Pink

### Ingredients
**Glass:**  whisky shot
**Mixers:** 40mL white crème de menthe
  1 teaspoon grenadine

### Method
Pour white crème de menthe followed by a dash of grenadine or raspberry cordial.

**Technique:** Shoot.

**Comments:** For those who are bashful when complimented.

# Towering Inferno

### Ingredients

**Glass:**   cordial (Embassy)

**Mixers:**   10mL dry gin
10mL triple sec
10mL green Chartreuse

### Method

Layer in order, then light.

**Technique:** Shoot while flaming.

**Comments:** Designed to set the night on fire.

# Traffic Light

## Ingredients

**Glass:**    tall Dutch cordial

**Mixers:**   10mL strawberry liqueur
        10mL Galliano
        25mL green Chartreuse

## Method

Layer in order, then light.

**Technique:** Suction-straw shoot.

**Comments:** Ready set go! Substitute banana liqueur for Galliano and melon liqueur for green Chartreuse, for those with a sweet tooth.

# U-Turn

## Ingredients

**Glass:** whisky shot

**Mixers:** 15mL banana liqueur
30mL Tia Maria

## Method

Layer in order.

**Technique:** Shoot.

**Comments:** The banana offers the curve yet its the Tia Maria that sends you around the bend. A complete change of direction.

# Vibrator

## Ingredients

**Glass:**   cordial (Embassy)
**Mixers:**  10mL Bailey's Irish Cream
             20mL Southern Comfort

## Method

Layer in order.

**Technique:** Shoot.

**Comments:** Batteries are not required for this stimulating and pulsating comfort.-

# Violet Slumber

## Ingredients

**Glass:**   cordial (Lexington)

**Mixers:**  15mL Malibu
10mL Parfait Amour
10mL orange juice

## Method

Layer in order.

**Technique:** Shoot.

**Comments:** Pretty to look at, better to drink, but don't slumber on this number.

# Vodka-Tini

### Ingredients

**Glass:**   cordial (Embassy)

**Mixers:** 25mL vodka
          1 teaspoon dry vermouth

### Method

Pour in order, then stir.

**Technique:** Shoot.

**Comments:** No olive is required. Preferably served chilled.

# Water-Bubba

### Ingredients

**Glass:**  cordial (Embassy)
**Mixers:**  10mL cherry advocaat
10mL advocaat
10mL blue curaçao

### Method

Pour advocaat into cherry advocaat, then layer the blue curaçao.

**Technique:** Shoot.

**Comments:** The advocaat resembles an egg yolk, with veins of cherry advocaat. Also known as an **"Unborn Baby"**.

# Andy Williams

## Ingredients

**Glass:** 290mL old-fashioned spirit glass

**Mixers:** 60mL Claytons tonic
15mL lime juice
dash sugar syrup
top up with soda water

## Method

Shake with ice and pour.

**Garnish:** Thin lime slice floated in drink.

**Comments:** A delightful pre-dinner drink.

# Andy's Passion

## Ingredients

**Glass:**  270mL hi-ball glass

**Mixers:** 90mL passionfruit pulp
90mL tropical juice
60mL natural yoghurt

## Method

Blend with ice and pour.

**Garnish:** Swizzle stick and straw.

**Comments:** A taste of sunshine with the unique tang of passionfruit.

# Apricot Smoothie

### Ingredients
**Glass:** 390mL poco grande glass
**Mixers:** 2 apricots
90mL milk
15mL lemon juice
30mL vanilla yoghurt

### Method
Blend with ice and pour.

**Garnish:** Apricot slice and straws.

**Comments:** A large smooth drink, with apricot flavour.

# Banana Bash

### Ingredients

**Glass:** 285mL hi-ball glass

**Mixers:** 1 ripe banana
4 raspberries
scoop vanilla ice cream
90mL tropical fruit juice

### Method

Blend with ice and pour.

**Garnish:** A sugar dusted raspberry on a banana wedge.

**Comments:** A great tasting blend of raspberry and banana.

# Banana Berry Smoothie

## Ingredients

**Glass:** 170mL champagne flute

**Mixers:** ⅓ ripe banana
60mL orange juice
3 tablespoons mixed berries

## Method

Blend with ice and pour.

**Garnish:** Straw.

**Comments:** Berry bonanza.

# Bell's Boomer

### Ingredients

**Glass:** 500mL fancy hi-ball glass

**Mixers:** 30mL apple juice
30mL orange juice
30mL grapefruit juice
30mL lime juice
125mL dry ginger ale

### Method

Build over ice.

**Garnish:** Half an orange slice, novelty and straw.

**Comments:** A large energising fruit drink, ideal before tackling those early morning breakers.

# Blushing Berry

## Ingredients

**Glass:** 260mL margarita glass

**Mixers:** 100mL milk
30mL raspberry cordial
60mL whipped cream
15mL coconut milk
frozen raspberries

## Method

Blend ice, raspberry cordial, coconut milk, milk and whipped cream.

**Garnish:** Place frozen raspberries around rim.

**Comments:** Created by Mary Jane Porta of Termo, Albury and was a finalist in the Best Border Beverage Competition.

# Bobby Dazzler

## Ingredients

**Glass:** 260mL poco grande glass

**Mixers:** 60mL grenadine
200mL cola
whipped cream
hundreds and thousands

## Method

Blend grenadine with ice and pour. Pour into glass, top with whipped cream and sprinkle with hundreds and thousands.

**Garnish:** Place strawberry on side and serve with swizzle stick and straw.

**Comments:** By Maxine Nash, Bubbles-Wodonga Hotel, was a runner-up in the Best Border Beverage Competition.

# Brazilian Breakdance

## Ingredients

**Glass:** 340mL poco grande glass

**Mixers:** 2 teaspoons instant coffee
scoop vanilla ice cream
125mL milk

## Method

Blend with ice and pour.

**Garnish:** Teaspoon of chocolate flakes.

**Comments:** A luscious, thick glass of iced coffee flavour, with just a hint of sweetness.

# Candy Bar

## Ingredients

**Glass:** 260mL poco grande glass

**Mixers:** 200mL milk
15mL chocolate topping
30mL caramel topping
whipped cream

## Method

Blend ice, milk chocolate and caramel topping.

**Garnish:** Top with whipped cream and sprinkle with icing sugar and shaved chocolate.

**Comments:** Created by Mary Ann Macure of Anthony's Restaurant, Wodonga and was a finalist in the Best Border Beverage Competition.

# Cane Toad

### Ingredients

**Glass:** 250mL fancy hi-ball glass

**Mixers:** 30mL passionfruit pulp
30mL sugar syrup
30mL lemon juice
top up with dry ginger ale

### Method

Shake with ice and pour.

**Garnish:** Two lemon slices and mint leaves.

**Comments:** A fizzy cane toad without the poison, a very refreshing tart drink.

# Carrot Wizz

### Ingredients

**Glass:** 200mL old-fashioned spirit glass

**Mixers:** 60mL tomato juice
½ medium carrot (thinly sliced)
dash horseradish sauce
dash lemon juice

### Method

Blend with ice and pour.

**Garnish:** Carrot top, floated on top.

**Comments:** "What's up Doc?" Created by Blaza Nikolic of the Hyatt Hotel, Melbourne.

# Chocolate Frog

## Ingredients

**Glass:**   360mL poco grande glass

**Mixers:**  250mL cola
             15mL chocolate topping
             dash peppermint essence
             whipped cream

## Method

Build over ice.

**Garnish:** Top with whipped cream, sprinkle with nutmeg and place sliced strawberry on side of glass. Serve with swizzle stick and straw.

**Comments:** By Annie Brouwer of Thermo-Albury and was a runner-up in the Best Border Beverage Competition.

# Claytons Sour

## Ingredients

**Glass:**  200mL bacchus wine glass

**Mixers:** 90mL Claytons
15mL sugar syrup
60mL lemon juice

## Method

Shake with ice and pour.

**Garnish:** Maraschino cherry.

**Comments:** Along the traditional lines.

# Clover Blossom

### Ingredients

**Glass:** 260mL hi-ball glass

**Mixers:** 60mL lemon cordial
30mL lime juice
1 egg white
dash grenadine
top up with tonic water

### Method

Blend with ice and pour.

**Garnish:** Lemon slice, mint leaf and straw.

**Comments:** A delicate fluffy concoction.

# Cock-A-Doodle

### Ingredients

**Glass:** 260mL salud grande glass

**Mixers:** 90mL dark grape juice
90mL lemon juice
15mL lime cordial
15mL sugar syrup
dash grenadine

### Method

Shake with ice and strain.

**Garnish:** Lime slice and dark grapes on side of glass.

**Comments:** Wake up to this little refresher.

# Coffee Crunch

## Ingredients

**Glass:** 400mL hurricane glass

**Mixers:** 90mL coconut cream
90mL cream
1 egg
125mL iced coffee

## Method

Blend with ice and pour.

**Garnish:** Sprinkle with cinnamon sugar, serve with straw and decorate as desired.

**Comments:** Created by Gaye Fendyke of Termo-Albury and was a runner-up in the Best Border Beverage Competition.

# Corio Bay Sunset

## Ingredients

**Glass:** 285mL hi-ball glass

**Mixers:** 4 large strawberries
30mL lime juice
125mL orange and mango juice
15mL Claytons
top up with lemonade

## Method

Blend with ice and strain.

**Garnish:** Orange slice.

**Comments:** A delightful combination of citrus and berry flavours.

# Corra Bear

## Ingredients

**Glass:** 285mL poco grande glass

**Mixers:** 200mL cola
30mL iced coffee
whipped cream

## Method

Build over ice and stir.

**Garnish:** Top with whipped cream and place maraschino cherry on top, with a slice of kiwi fruit on side of glass. Serve with straws.

**Comments:** Created by Mary Jane Porta of Termo, Albury and was outright winner of the Best Border Beverages Competition.

# Creamy Banana

## Ingredients

**Glass:** 360mL fiesta grande glass

**Mixers:** 1 ripe banana, sliced
30mL coconut cream
60mL milk
scoop vanilla ice cream

## Method

Blend with ice and strain.

**Garnish:** Sprinkle with chocolate flakes.

**Comments:** A delicate creamy drink.

# Dick Little

## Ingredients

**Glass:**   360mL fancy hi-ball glass

**Mixers:**  60mL apricot nectar
15mL lime juice
top up with bitter lemon

## Method

Build over ice.

**Garnish:** Lemon slices on side of glass, swizzle stick and straw.

# Doctor's Orders

## Ingredients

**Glass:** 260mL salud grande glass

**Mixers:** 30mL lime juice
125mL grapefruit juice
2 sachets Lite-n-Low, or Equal
top up with tonic water

## Method

Shake with ice and strain.

**Garnish:** Lime slice and straws.

**Comments:** A juice a day to keep the doctor away.

# Fruit Mocquiri

### Ingredients

**Glass:**   250mL margarita glass

**Mixers:**  60mL strawberries, peaches or mango

15mL sugar syrup

15mL lemon juice

30mL apple juice

### Method

Blend with ice and pour.

**Garnish:** Small slice of the ingredient fruit.

**Comments:** A smooth rich blend of your favourite fruit. I particularly like mango, as used in the photograph above.

# Fruit Squash

## Ingredients

**Glass:** 285mL hi-ball glass

**Mixers:** 2 strawberries
4 raspberries
tablespoon crushed pineapple
tablespoon passionfruit pulp
½ kiwifruit
60mL orange juice

## Method

Blend with ice and pour.

**Garnish:** Berry studded pineapple spear.

**Comments:** A fruit lovers delight.

# Gator

## Ingredients

**Glass:** 170mL champagne flute

**Mixers:** 90mL grapefruit juice
30mL lime cordial

## Method

Build over ice.

**Garnish:** Lime peel curl.

**Comments:** Sharp and tangy aperitif.

# Ginger Mick

## Ingredients

**Glass:** 290mL old-fashioned spirit glass

**Mixers:** 125mL dry ginger ale
15mL lime juice
30mL Claytons tonic
30mL lemon juice
60mL apple juice

## Method

Stir with ice.

**Garnish:** Apple peel threaded inside glass, with lemon slice on side with mint sprig.

**Comments:** A thirst quenching drink to combat the summer sun.

# Health Farm

## Ingredients

**Glass:** 260mL hi-ball glass

**Mixers:** 90mL pineapple juice
2 slices rockmelon
90mL orange juice
2 teaspoons honey
½ ripe banana

## Method

Blend with ice and pour.

**Garnish:** Rockmelon wedge and swizzle stick.

**Comments:** A great drink for the health conscious. Created by Wayne Baker of Tousson Restaurant, Geelong.

# Henry VIII

## Ingredients

**Glass:** 200mL old-fashioned spirit glass

**Mixers:** 60mL apple juice
15mL lemon juice
top up with dry ginger ale
½ teaspoon of grenadine

## Method

Build over ice.

**Garnish:** To finish, gently add grenadine to top.

**Comments:** A very piquant and gingery drink, suitable for afternoon relaxation.

# Iron Man

## Ingredients
**Glass:** 360mL fancy hi-ball glass
**Mixers:** 1 egg
45mL honey
1 ripe banana, sliced
150mL orange juice

## Method
Blend with ice and pour.

**Garnish:** A vanilla bean floated, then sprinkle flaked chocolate over top.

**Comments**: Choc-a-block with energy.

# Island Paradise

## Ingredients

**Glass:** 90mL martini glass

**Mixers:** 30mL orange juice
15mL coconut cream
30mL lime juice
dash sugar syrup

## Method

Shake with ice and strain.

**Garnish:** Lime slice and sprig of mint.

**Comments:** Tropical tastes in a short and piquant thirst-quencher.

# Issy Wassy

## Ingredients

**Glass:** 250mL hurricane glass

**Mixers:** 125mL milk
½ banana
2 slices rockmelon

## Method

Blend with ice and pour.

**Garnish:** Rockmelon slice with straws.

**Comments:** For the smooth stylish chap.

# Jaffa

## Ingredients

**Glass:**  170mL old-fashioned spirit glass
**Mixers:**  scoop chocolate ice cream
          90mL orange juice

## Method

Blend with ice and pour.

**Garnish:** 1 teaspoon grated chocolate on top.

**Comments:** Just like a liquid jaffa.

# Jersey Cow

## Ingredients

**Glass:** 260mL old-fashioned spirit glass

**Mixers:** 180mL cola
scoop chocolate ice cream

## Method

Stir over ice.

**Garnish:** Teaspoon of grated chocolate over top.

**Comments:** A choc-cola delight.

# Jimmy's Beach Cruiser

## Ingredients

**Glass:**  380mL viva grande glass

**Mixers:**  6 raspberries

2 tablespoons crushed pineapple

60mL orange juice

top up with lemonade

## Method

Blend with ice and pour.

**Garnish:** Two raspberries on side of glass, plus optional decoration.

**Comments:** A great blend of flavours.

# Joh's Country

## Ingredients

**Glass:** 360mL fiesta grande glass

**Mixers:** 45mL pineapple juice
30mL coconut cream
dash lime cordial
60mL mango and orange juice

## Method

Blend with ice and pour.

**Garnish:** Mango slice, straw and optional decoration.

**Comments:** Rich, creamy, coconut flavour.

# Juice Combo

## Ingredients

**Glass:** 250mL footed hi-ball glass

**Mixers:** 45mL pineapple juice
45mL orange juice
45mL apple juice
45mL dark grape juice
30mL lime juice
15mL sugar syrup

## Method

Build over ice and stir.

**Garnish:** Two dark grapes on side of glass.

**Comments:** A refreshing blend of juices.

# Julie's Black Cat

### Ingredients
**Glass:**   260mL hi-ball glass
**Mixers:**  15mL lemon juice
            125mL dark grape juice
            60mL lemonade
            60mL dry ginger ale

### Method
Build over ice.

**Garnish:** Lemon twists dropped in glass, straw and optional decoration.

**Comments:** Let this one cross your path, a dry tasty drink.

# Kate's Pink Echidna

### Ingredients

**Glass:**  285mL hi-ball glass

**Mixers:** 3 strawberries
2 slices rockmelon
30mL sugar syrup
dash lemon juice
top up with lemonade

### Method

Blend with ice and pour.

**Garnish:** Rockmelon slice and strawberry on side of glass.

**Comments:** A delicate melon flavour.

# Lethal Weapon

## Ingredients

**Glass:** 285mL hi-ball glass

**Mixers:** 200mL V8 juice
1 teaspoon hot chilli sauce
salt and pepper
15mL lemon juice

## Method

Build over ice and stir.

**Garnish:** Celery stalk.

**Comments:** Full of vitamins, but with a fiery bite at the end.
A great heart starter at breakfast time.

# Mickey Mouse

## Ingredients

**Glass:** 285mL hi-ball glass

**Mixers:** 90mL orange juice
30mL raspberry cordial
90mL lemonade

## Method

Build over ice.

**Garnish:** Two cherries on side of glass.

**Comments:** A dash of vitamin C for your sweet tooth.

# Mintlup

## Ingredients

**Glass:** 285mL hi-ball glass

**Mixers:** large sprig of crushed mint
15mL lime juice
90mL dry ginger ale
90mL lemon and lime mineral water

## Method

Build over ice.

**Garnish:** Mint leaf on lemon slice.

**Comments:** Southern hospitality in prohibition days perhaps.

# Mocktini

## Ingredients

**Glass:** 90mL martini glass

**Mixers:** 15mL lime juice
dash lemon juice
60mL tonic water

## Method

Stir with ice and strain.

**Garnish:** A green olive on a toothpick or a lemon twist.

**Comments:** A non-alcoholic version of the classic cocktail.

# Mocquiri

## Ingredients
**Glass:**   90mL martini glass
**Mixers:**  60mL apple juice
15mL lemon juice
15mL sugar syrup

## Method
Blend with ice and strain.

**Garnish:** Lemon or lime twist.

**Comments:** An apple flavoured non-alcoholic daiquiri.

# Oramato

## Ingredients
**Glass:** 250mL footed hi-ball glass
**Mixers:** 90mL tomato juice
125mL orange juice

## Method
Shake with ice and pour.

**Garnish:** Orange peel curl.

**Comments:** Try this orange tomato combo for a taste difference.

# Peach Magic

## Ingredients

**Glass:**  400mL hurricane glass

**Mixers:**  1 peach or apricot, stoned
90mL orange and mango juice
90mL apple juice
top up with dry ginger ale

## Method

Build over ice and pour.

**Garnish:** Watermelon slice and stemmed maraschino cherry.

**Comments:** A large refreshing taste of the orchard.

# Pina Con Nada

## Ingredients

**Glass:**   260mL footed hi-ball glass

**Mixers:**  90mL pineapple juice
30mL coconut cream
15mL sugar syrup

## Method

Blend with ice and pour.

**Garnish:** Wedge of pineapple and a strawberry with straws.

**Comments:** The creamy non-alcoholic version of the famous Pina Colada.

# Shirley Temple

## Ingredients

**Glass:** 285mL hi-ball glass

**Mixers:** 15mL grenadine

top up with ginger ale or lemonade

## Method

Build over ice.

**Garnish:** Slice of orange, serve with swizzle stick and two straws.

**Comments:** For a tangy variation to this drink try a Shirley Temple No.2. Use the following: 60mL pineapple juice to a glass half full of ice. Top with lemonade, float 15mL passionfruit pulp on top and garnish with a pineapple wedge and cherry.

# Shrinking Violet

## Ingredients

**Glass:**  260mL hi-ball glass

**Mixers:**  125mL dark grape juice
90mL lemonade
15mL lime juice

## Method

Build with ice and stir.

**Garnish:** Two dark grapes and straw.

**Comments:** A light but sharp drink.

# Spazz

## Ingredients

**Glass:**   285mL hi-ball glass
**Mixers:**  ½ peach or apricot, stoned
            150mL pineapple juice
            15mL lime juice

## Method

Blend with ice and pour.

**Garnish:** Pour a teaspoon of grenadine over top of drink, add apricot slice and straw.

**Comments:** A long, delicately flavoured drink.

# Strawberry Zappie

### Ingredients

**Glass:** 285mL hi-ball glass

**Mixers:** 4 strawberries
180mL apple juice
30mL lemon juice
dash lime cordial

### Method

Blend with ice and pour.

**Garnish:** Small strawberry on straw.

**Comments:** A sharp, tasty refresher.

# Sundowner

## Ingredients

**Glass:** 200mL old-fashioned spirit glass

**Mixers:** 75mL orange juice and mango Juice
15mL lemon juice
45mL Clayton's tonic

## Method

Shake with ice and pour.

**Garnish:** Lemon slice, floated

**Comment:** A citrus tang to activate the taste buds.

# Sydneysider

## Ingredients
**Glass:** 360mL fiesta grande glass

**Mixers:** 30mL lemon juice
30mL orange juice
30mL grapefruit juice
30mL pineapple juice
60mL apple juice
½ egg white
dash grenadine

## Method
Shake with ice and pour.

**Garnish:** Apple fan.

**Comments:** Fruit medley in the Opera House.

# Virgin Maria

## Ingredients
**Glass:** 250mL footed hi-ball glass
**Mixers:** 180mL tomato juice
         dash lemon juice
         15mL hot chilli sauce

## Method
Blend with ice and pour.

**Garnish:** Cucumber slice, cherry tomatoes and optional decoration.

**Comments:** A very hot and spicy drink, guaranteed to keep you that way.

# Virgin Mary

## Ingredients
**Glass:** 270mL hi-ball glass

**Mixers:** 150mL tomato juice
15mL lemon juice
teaspoon Worcestershire sauce
2–3 drops Tabasco sauce
salt and pepper to taste

## Method
Build over ice and stir.

**Garnish:** Celery stalk, lemon slice and straws.

**Comments:** A spicy refreshing start to the day.

# Index

## Cocktail index

# Index

# Index

## Shooters index

# Index

# Index

## Non-alcoholic index